# PABLO'S WAR

# PABLO'S WAR

SQUADRON LEADER PABLO MASON

with Kim Bartlett

WARNER BOOKS

A *Warner* Book

First published in Great Britain in 1992 by Bloomsbury
This edition published by Warner Books in 1993
Reprinted 1993, 1994, 1995

A CIP catalogue record for this book
is available from the British Library

ISBN 0 7515 0395 9

Typeset by Hewer Text Composition Services, Edinburgh
Printed in England by Clays Ltd, St Ives plc

Warner Books
A Division of
Little, Brown and Company (UK)
Brettenham House
Lancaster Place
London WC2E 7EN

For Michael and Eleanor

# Contents

# Contents

# Introduction

Looking back now I can see how much my life has changed. Just days after I came home from the Gulf a very dear friend did her best to explain to me that my new and very different attitude to life would change again when I reached her age. It angered me to think that anyone who had not lived through the past few months alongside me dared to assume that only the maturity of age would ever grant me a proper perspective on life. I had just lived through an experience that would change my values for ever. Age had nothing to do with my learning process, but how could I possibly explain the true realities of the war I had just fought? There had been many moments over the past few months when I felt sure I was about to die; I had often measured my life in terms of days or even just a few hours. I am still not certain how I feel about that time, but I have discovered that the many things that happened to me during the first few months of 1991 have changed my future for ever.

# 1

# The First Mission

Just after 1.30 a.m. on 17 January 1991 President Bush's final Gulf War deadline was still only a few hours old and we were all nervously aware that we were breaking new and dangerous ground. I knew what worried all my flying team was the fear that this crucial moment in our lives had passed and that if nothing else happened we would just carry on training to an already perfected plan. For we were like athletes or finely tuned animals, trained to our peak and ready for the race, only to be told it had been postponed. But I knew we could not keep up that pace indefinitely – something just had to give. Yet at the same time we nurtured the desperate hope that, despite the fact that the deadline had passed, the political brinkmanship would continue and somehow save us all from the awful prospect of fighting this war.

To me it was simple: all the politicians had to do was to persuade the Iraqis that any hostility on their part would be absolutely futile. The Iraqis didn't stand a chance; I knew it and they must have known it too. Were they really a nation with some weird family tree that linked them to the Japanese Kamikaze pilots of the Second World War, who confused honour with dying? Did Saddam Hussein really care so little for his people? Or did he care so much for national pride that he was prepared to sacrifice them in their tens of thousands for absolutely nothing?

I had always believed that a peaceful solution was just around the corner. Maybe it was arrogance, but I could never accept that anyone would be crazy enough to take on the biggest and most powerful air and land armada ever assembled. My belief in the sheer folly of that confrontation sustained my hopes of peace until the very last moment.

We all piled into the waiting coach for the twenty-minute ride to the airfield. I still felt relaxed as I heard my boys joking. It would be an easy day, since we had already flown a mirror image of our planned sortie only the day before, and if all attempts at peace failed, it would be the one we would fly to war with.

The boys piled off the coach at our Muharraq base, in Bahrain, and as they disappeared behind the wall of sandbags to change into flying kit I made my way into the intelligence HQ. There my heart stopped, for I saw Nick Heard, my deputy back at our Laarbruch base in north Germany, blocking my way in the narrow makeshift passageway. I tried to catch his eye, but in the shadowy half-light I could see he was miles away, deep in thought, and clearly he didn't even realize I was there. I walked right up to him and cautiously asked: 'What's up, mate?' He

2

barely whispered his reply: 'We're going . . . we're bloody well GOING!'

I recoiled. His words were already bouncing around in my head but my brain was numb. All at once I felt a terrible, sickening fear for myself, for my team and for all our families. I had trained very hard with all seven boys in my team, and we worked well together, but I hoped we would never have to die together. Yet fear was swirling around in some crazy cocktail with jubilation and relief that finally, after so many build-ups and disappointments, we were going to war. At last we were going to do the job we had been so meticulously trained to do, and then it would be all over.

It was obvious that Nick could not talk to me and now I felt just the same: I didn't want to be touched or spoken to as I stumbled, almost blindly, into the intelligence cell. It was a hive of activity, since the first formation from my squadron were already preparing to lead the way into battle. They were the lads to take eight of our fast jets on the first bombing wave, and they didn't need me around. I walked out, heading for my own flying kit and to where my boys would be waiting. Had they heard the news? Or would I have to tell them all that this was finally it? I had only to look at the tension on their faces as they sat around in the cramped space: there I recognized the same mixture of anxiety, awe, anticipation and relief, and I too was relieved.

I needed to check my own thoughts, just to be sure that I had understood what was happening. Surely this was only part of our final training. We had left the hotel that morning as we had every day so far, and none of us had felt any different. Besides, our plans couldn't be changed now: my navigator, Gary Stapleton, and another pilot, John Peters, had arranged to play tennis at lunchtime while I umpired and drank Pimms.

But it had all changed, and I found myself putting on my war suit. It was the regular khaki flying suit we had all been issued with, bearing my rank braid and a Union Jack Velcroed over my left breast. But underneath, for the first time in eight years, I was wearing a very old and frayed red Coca-Cola T-shirt. It was full of little black holes burned through the shoulders and chest, and Sheila, my wife, had tried many times to throw it out. I had always managed to rescue it, sometimes in the nick of time as the dustcart pulled up outside our home, and once from a local Boy Scouts' jumble sale. Something inside me was sure that one day that T-shirt would be needed; now I knew why.

It had saved my life once. I knew it had because I should have been killed back in 1983. It was 29 July and I had just completed my tactical weapons training course at RAF Chivenor in Devon. After the course I hung around in the crewroom on the scrounge for any extra sorties so that I could keep my hand in before my conversion to flying Tornadoes. On one of those sorties that day a student pilot flew right into me, completely smashing up both jets.

We all managed to eject, and I escaped with a few burns and bruises. But the red T-shirt was peppered with shot from the explosive charges in the aircraft's canopy and my ejection seat rockets, which, with only microseconds to spare, had jettisoned me safely as the jet broke up around me.

The inquiry that followed found that the crash had been entirely the young and inexperienced foreign student's fault. Soon afterwards he flew home to Baghdad to become a fighter pilot – in the Iraqi Air Force.

When I left for the Gulf in December 1990 I packed that old T-shirt in my bag, not really thinking why. Something drew me to it but I couldn't work it out. Today it was going to become my bullet-proof vest, my psychological suit of armour. I never flew without it again. Every one of us had something he believed would give him some extra and invisible protection. One of the guys, Glynn Harley, wore the same pair of unwashed socks on fourteen battle missions. Then he dared to wash them before flying again and when he came back unscathed it was almost with a sigh of relief. He had run the risk of washing those socks and survived, so it was OK to wash them. I finally washed my tatty talisman a month after flying into battle, since I had figured the old T-shirt too could take the risk.

Superstition ran high among us, every one a professional and highly skilled bomber pilot or navigator. Another flyer, Colin Ayton, always wore his Ray-Ban Aviator sunglasses for take-off and landing, even in the middle of a pitch-black night. Nor would he have climbed into the cockpit of his Tornado if he had not followed his usual routine of boarding our bus to travel just the few feet to where his jet would be waiting.

The aircraft were dispersed all over the airfield to reduce the devastating effects of an air attack and the bus was intended to ferry crews out to them. Had Colin's Tornado been parked right outside the operations block, he would still have boarded the bus. To walk those few feet and break that routine would have seemed like taking a stupid and unnecessary risk.

Our internal clocks were ticking impatiently and even the routine operations around the base had changed speed. Everything was moving faster, and just looking around I could see a visible transition to the pace of war. Over the last few days, it was true, you could feel that tempers had become frayed; everyone was working with a slightly shorter fuse. But something always came along to offer some temporary relief from the incredible tension.

One of the ground crew handed me my kit and cracked a well-worn but favourite joke about the weather. 'Turned out nice again, Sir,' he said as he politely stood by while I checked my kit. Of course it was nice. This was the desert, for God's sake. We hadn't even seen a cloud for six weeks! But no one could resist the same crack at least once a day and that too became an essential part of our life-saving ritual.

The moment of fun was soon over and later, as I walked out to my waiting jet just a few hours before daybreak, the joke took on a sickening reality. I realized that on what would soon be another beautiful, bright-blue morning I was going to war.

Our first mission had already been carefully planned and few of us ever needed the maps and detailed written instructions we always took with us on each raid, for we had mentally flown to war many times. I can only vaguely recall listening to the roar of sixteen Tornado engines opening up to maximum reheat as the first formation took off into the dark. Our minds were full of what we had to do and we could only worry about our own uncertain future.

In the space of just a couple of hours I was already experiencing new thoughts and new emotions. I was forty years old and the intensity of those feelings came to me as a great shock. Vivid, scarcely imaginable ideas ran through my head as I methodically went through my final preparations.

During that countdown to war there was still time to snatch a few moments to be by myself. I sat down in a corner of our ops room and wrote a letter to Sheila and our children, Mike and Ellie. Everything I was feeling poured on to the paper through my pen. As the minutes to take-off ticked away I had no trouble getting down the final words of tenderness I wanted to say to my loved ones at home.

This was to be my last letter to them. During the build-up to war I had sometimes written as many as four airmail letters a day, but that was now over. I could not write to my family again, although I'm still not absolutely sure why. I tried to explain everything I felt for them and I will never forget those few sad words, for they came from my heart:

The Gulf

My Dearest Family,

I'm not really sure where I'm going, or why. I only know that I have to go. I couldn't live with myself, let alone anyone else, if I didn't do what I just have to do.

Whether or not I return is in the hands of God or whoever. If you ever read this it will be because I am never coming home.

Sheila,

Never forget that I died doing what I was very good at – and never forget that I loved every minute of it – that was flying. Whatever happened it would certainly have been very quick and painless.

Ellie,

Continue to grow as the beautiful young lady that you already are.

Mike,

Stay as strong as you were when I left home. The girls will need a man about the house and someone like you to take care of them . . .

I Love You All.

I just thank God this was a letter that Sheila never received, since it was for her to read and to show to my children if I did not come back. When I had sealed up my envelope I looked around the room to see some of my boys sitting alone, looking into space, while others scribbled little notes which they then tucked away. Fortunately, like mine, these never had to be opened.

When I came back from that first mission I

retrieved my own letter, which I had left for safe-keeping with all my personal belongings. I took it back to my hotel room and tore it into tiny pieces before burning the remains to ash. Whatever happened now, Sheila would never read that letter.

Everything had been planned to the last second weeks before. We knew by heart the maps and detailed data for every mission. But by the time we were ready to go we had gone through everything again right up until the last possible moment.

The briefing room was as quiet as a graveyard. There was still five minutes to go to final brief, but everyone on my team was there. Unsteadily, I focused on the briefing board, which was festooned with maps, photographs of enemy territory and military sites and endless intelligence data. Slowly I stood up to address my team before taking them to war. As I turned to face them I could feel seven pairs of anxious eyes almost burning through to the back of my head. I whispered a barely audible time-check, and then made a mental note to speak up the next time. But I had passed my own personal test as I issued final instructions: inside I was shaking like jelly but as I held out my hand to check my wristwatch my arm remained perfectly still. As everyone else checked theirs, I suddenly wondered how many of us would come back. Had they all even found the guts to go? Dare I ask myself if *I* could?

Our first bombing raid was to hit an airfield deep behind enemy lines. We had planned to fly to the target in darkness but we would be running for home in broad daylight. The plan was delayed by a couple of hours, which meant we would be going both ways without the reassuring veil of night. Finally, with our last brief over, I had built up my own mental map of all the known enemy threats *en route*.

We were then handed our Walther PP handguns, each loaded with a magazine of eight rounds. I suddenly wondered if I would have the courage to save the last bullet for myself. Chris Lunt must have read my mind as he joked across the ops room, 'You'd probably miss anyway, Dad.' Then we all laughed as he added, 'Even if you didn't, it would just bounce off your thick skull!'

All the planning and intelligence staff who had helped prepare our mission slowly shuffled out of the room. Most of them would stop and look back at someone they had come to see as a dear friend. Some muttered good wishes but few could look any of us in the eye. We were all scared together. Four Tornadoes would carry eight aircrew to war and, hopefully, bring us all safely home, yet there were dozens more who would mentally fly every second of that mission with us. It was terrible for them too.

With just over an hour to go, it was time for the dreaded 'sterilization' process, a procedure we knew we would have to carry out but all hated. A pretty WRAF officer nervously held out a plastic bag, into which I put my last letter to my family, my handkerchief, a small notebook, my wallet and a couple of pens. Only essential kit could be taken to war, since a skilled enemy interrogator could learn much from our personal possessions.

I fought back tears as I pulled off my thick gold wedding band – the next day it would be my sixteenth wedding anniversary. Then, for the first time in my life, I removed the battered gold signet ring that had been a sixteenth-birthday present from my wife. We were childhood sweethearts and here I was putting twenty-four years of my life in a damned polythene bag.

All the aircrew carried a number of gold sovereigns, escape maps printed on silk and a 'goolie chit': a letter written in English and in Arabic promising a £15,000 reward if a captured flyer was returned to safety still 'white and serviceable'. I knew that few of us were as scared of being killed in combat as we were of being shot down and taken prisoner. We were about to fight a very clinical war. It would be a battle where we all knew that suddenly any one of us might no longer exist.

Our greatest fear was to eject and be captured and tortured; there was an awful horror at the thought of being forced to suffer terribly. No one wanted to die. The bottom line was that you wanted to live and never have to suffer pain. Every one of us had at some stage in the past few days quizzed our intelligence advisers about how we might be treated by the enemy if we were shot down alive. The answer was always very brief: 'Badly.'

We zipped ourselves into our thigh-hugging anti-gravity corsets, buttoned on our blast-resisting life-jackets and checked all the screws and plugs that, like umbilical cords, would attach us to the aircraft. Gary Stapleton checked my kit and I checked his, but there was no need: no one would be flying today in kit that had not been scrutinized by our ground crew a dozen times already.

The tension that had been building up to one climax after another was suddenly broken when the Scottish flyer Colin Ayton, 'Stroppy Jock' to the rest of us, called out in his daft mock-American drawl, 'Lookin' good and feelin' keen, I'm a lean, mean fightin' machine.' I was glad my lads were buoyed up by their own high spirits.

I checked my kit again to be sure I was carrying everything I believed could help save my life. My pockets were crammed with sachets of water, a wire hacksaw blade was sewn into my flying suit and a pocket compass was hidden in one of its elbows. A cloth soaked with orange juice and then dried out was tucked into the lining of my collar. We all had our own personal survival extras. I worked out that if I needed to eject I could disguise any foul-tasting water by soaking it with my orange-juice-impregnated rag. At the end of the war I tried it out and it was perfectly disgusting.

Then I lifted my helmet from its peg, carefully removing the soft velvet cover from the visor. I checked the visor was clean, since what might look like a scratch could instantly become an enemy fighter, poised and microseconds from the kill. Gently I replaced the cover over the gleaming visor. There would be no spectral fighters out there today – just the real thing. There were just minutes to go before we would leave the last sanctuary of the ops room, and I could see the supreme confidence gleaming in everyone's eyes. Then Mike Toft lifted our spirits a notch higher as he cracked another favourite line of ours from the TV comedy *Blackadder Goes Forth*, assuring us all that we would be 'back in time for tea and medals'. This was still the RAF all right. We may have been decades on, but we all still believed in the values that carried so many brave flyers through the First and Second World Wars.

Almost as soon as I felt sure that my emotions were completely under control, I would feel another wave of regret and disappointment wash over me. There were sad thoughts of having wasted so much time in my life. When everything that was left for me could be over within seconds, the eternity behind me seemed to me to have been so terribly wasted. Why hadn't I painted that garage door before I flew out to the Gulf? The prospect that in a few moments I might not exist made me regret not having done so many things when in fact I had so much time in my life.

I would never have believed that the concept of time could take on such enormous significance. From the very first mission, the few seconds that it took to bomb a heavily defended target could suddenly expand into hours. Then several hours waiting for the next take-off on a bombing sortie would disappear in moments. Time for me has never settled back into that reassuring pattern of seconds becoming minutes which in turn become hours. I know that time can be elastic; I have experienced it.

As we waited in those early hours of darkness I

could see that some of my men needed to be alone with their private thoughts and fears, while others would be seeking out encouragement to steel them through the next few hours of life or death. I had planned our sortie so that we walked out to our waiting aircraft one hour before take-off. For me the tension that had by now become unbearable would dissipate as I walked out to my jet, leaving everything but my mission behind.

It was yet another distortion of time. Before we went to war the clock seemed to have speeded up as we accelerated towards self-destruction, but that last hour before take-off was gone in seconds as though it had vaporized with the heat from our jet engines. As I focused on every task throughout the war, the pressure of concentration built up into a massive crescendo, but every time I reached what I believed was a new and even higher level I would burst right through it in a never-ending ascent.

The boys were ready and it was time to go. There was nothing more we could do but fly to war. I reached for the door handle, determined that no one but me would open the polythene bag filled with my dearest possessions. I *would* bring every one of us home safe and sound. But the door burst open in front of me and I was face to face with a triumphant team who had just successfully returned from the very first mission of the war.

Squadron Leader Gordon Buckley came crashing into the ops room. His lined face was etched with the stains of a close-fitting oxygen mask and the grime of a good night's work. Gordon sprawled towards

14

me and my team, bundled ahead by a tidal wave of jubilant followers. There was elation and a few tears, for they had gone out and all come home safely. Gordon's face creased into a huge, confident smile as he shouted to me, 'Awesome . . . effin' awesome . . . we were effin' awesome!'

I didn't want to look at them or listen to their war cries. There were two very different teams now crowded into a narrow corridor but we might just as well have been a million miles apart. They were battle-hardened, tried-and-tested war veterans who had gone out and come back successful from their very first mission. They had found the guts to go, yet we had still to find them. We were still virgin warriors.

I'll never forget the victory cries: gentle Rupert Clark, who could have been telling the whole world how his mission had 'run on rails', and others announcing that it was 'nice to see the dawn come up', or confidently inquiring, 'Have they given up yet?' I felt intensely jealous of young men who had had less than a year on the squadron and yet had tasted war, whereas I was still to experience what these 'old hands' had already been through.

Nor will I ever forget the moment Gordon Buckley offered me kind and thoughtful reassurance by patting me firmly on the back and saying, 'It's easy, you'll sail through. I'll see you later.' I wished he hadn't done that to me. Their success made me question my own ability to get my boys back safely. Perhaps in some way their incredible good luck somehow diminished our own chances.

The corridor was half-full of jubilant, confident aircrew. My team of eight men, including myself, filled the other half; uncertain, cautious and deeply envious. I was witnessing history in the making and I was part of it. I needed to get my boys out, because we didn't want to hear their wonderful war stories; we wanted to be able to tell our own. There were so many conflicting emotions struggling for supremacy in my mind and time was fast running out in which to rationalize them all.

Ours was Mission 1501G. As we walked shoulder to shoulder out to our jets I was already feeling much better. I had left my loved ones, Sheila and the kids, back there in the ops room. There were fewer butterflies in my stomach, more pride and less doubt. Who on earth would ever dare to take us on? I was one of the best of the best and the world had to know it. We were the new warriors and it was our turn to go to war.

Our ground crews were clearly nervous as we walked out to them in the half-light: we would be flying their aircraft not our own. Every Tornado was the personal property and responsibility of the men who worked on them. The jet we flew would be simply on loan to us and all four jets on my mission would be handed back within hours.

Everything seemed tuned to perfection. I had walked around my aircraft and I trusted her and the men who took such loving care of her. Gary checked over his navigation systems, and then we calmly shook hands before we climbed up into the cockpit and closed the canopy. We shook hands before every one of the nineteen war missions we flew together; it became vitally important to me. Everything apart from reaching our target and then getting home again became unimportant. Even my family were now hidden away somewhere out of my thoughts. It had been a great relief to leave the thought of them behind in the ops room and they never flew with me again.

We had checked and rechecked everything. Gary switched on his systems and we were ready to go, but this time we knew we would not be bringing back the eight 1000-lb bombs we were carrying. Our task was to disrupt enemy air operations from an airfield deep inside Iraq. The sun was already rising and I was faced with the terrible realization that I could already see the curvature of the earth. I would be able to see for hundreds of miles in this clear daylight and that meant that the enemy would also be able to see me.

Now there were just forty minutes left before take-off and I heard the joky but well-meant assurances from the ground crew as they encouragingly whispered, 'Give 'em one for me, Sir.' But they also wanted to offer us tremendous care that made us feel that we were each being treated as someone very special.

As we were being strapped into the jet there were always the reassuring words: 'This one won't let you down, Sir' or 'She'll take care of you – I checked her over myself.' Whenever a jet failed to get home the ground crew just would not believe it would not be appearing very soon over the horizon. A few of them could always be found hanging around in the aircraft dispersal area, refusing to accept that their Tornado would not come home. They would stay around for hours, sweeping up and busying themselves with pointless little tasks, waiting in the vain hope of hearing a familiar thundering sound in the distance.

I could have cried for them sometimes; it was pitiful to see the awful guilt they were suffering. They felt they had let you down in some very personal way by sending you to war in a jet that failed to bring you home, even if it had been shot down by enemy fire. There were mechanics and technicians who were convinced that if they had been more thorough, that Tornado would have miraculously escaped and come home.

No one ever relaxed until we were all safely back at base; even if there was an air-raid warning there would be ground crew who refused to take cover in a shelter. It was their job to stay and wait until we were home and they would carry that out whatever the risk to their own lives.

I had not smoked for eight years until I went to war, then after every one of my missions Sergeant Tom Armstrong would be the first man at the steps to my Tornado, waiting with a lighted Marlboro. We weren't just a team – we were a huge extended family, and our individual lives were inextricably linked.

Minutes before take-off my number three in the formation, Chris Lunt and Colin Ayton, reported a serious malfunction. But there was nothing we could do for them – they would have to stay behind. I could hear their voices over the radio change from

18

desperate hope that their jet could be fixed, to utter dejection that they would not be flying with us. I could also hear in their voices that they believed they had let the side down. I know that they would have tried anything to get airborne, but some of the controls were affected and their jet would have been a pig to fly. I considered the risks were unacceptable. I wanted brave men on my team but I didn't want brave dead men.

We finally took off as a three-ship formation for a four-hour sortie and one of those hours involved flying over enemy territory. We planned to travel at medium level – just a few thousand feet – refuelling about eight tons of fuel from the Victor tankers waiting on our way in to the target. It was a lot easier than I had imagined, since we were flying over familiar desert territory, but our sensitive radar was picking up sporadic warning attacks. They were false alarms, for we were still over friendly airspace, but the threats took on a new and deadly meaning because this time we were really going to war.

My sense of vulnerability was incredible, since I could see for hundreds of miles, and as we went in to refuel I knew with all our bombs on board we were heavier and far less agile than we had been used to being. My team was one of the lucky ones: they had all refuelled with extra weight on board at least once in their careers. But I had no doubt that others would be trying this out for the very first time.

In-flight refuelling is not an easy job and in the comfort of the mess we had often joked about how difficult it really was. Was it like trying to have sex

19

with a doughnut rolling down the runway, or was it like trying to shove spaghetti up a wild cat's backside? This time our refuelling went smoothly and we were on our way. Minutes later we headed for the enemy border and dropped to a comfortable low level of about 200ft to avoid being picked up by enemy long-range radar. Approaching the border, we went faster and lower.

As we crossed the border we were doing 600mph and at only 30ft off the ground we were going just as fast and as low as we dared. I had never flown that low in my whole life and I could not have got my jet down any lower. There was not much between the bottom of my jet and the ground – just a few feet – and I could feel the rush of air through the space in between.

It was like flying in a goldfish bowl with all the eyes of the enemy on me. On this huge, concave landscape I was hiding in gullies and ducking around sand dunes where enemy radar would never find me, but I felt as exposed as if I was being watched on national television.

The tension was incredible and the adrenalin raced through us as we flew within five minutes of our first deadly target. Then someone managed to call out on our secure radio, 'Is everybody happy?' We were fifteen minutes into enemy territory and we all sang back in unison, 'You bet your life we are!' Then I transmitted to the others that the joke was over. All I said was, 'OK guys, it's time to go to work.' No more needed to be said – we all understood and our concentration took over again.

We had seen specks on the landscape that were just cactus or a few camels, and we had passed over Bedouin tents with their camels and goats tethered all around, but we carried on flying as fast and as low as we dared. If those specks had been enemy missiles it would have been too late to change direction. I couldn't believe it when those desert people came out of their tents and actually waved to us. We didn't so much fly past their tents as fly round them and we didn't know whether to strafe them with bullets or wave back. We did neither.

Then we were running in to our target. There it was on the radar bright and clear and my finger was ready to let my bombs go. We were bang on target as I pressed the weapons-release button, letting go my 8000lb of bombs. Dropping them meant leaving the sanctuary of ultra-low-level flying, and two minutes later life started to get very interesting indeed. It seemed that no sooner had my hand twitched on the weapons release than all hell broke loose.

The sky suddenly changed as though someone was pulling a dark curtain across my eyes. If I could stay in the clear blue I would be all right. I had never seen anti-aircraft artillery before, but as the tracers threaded their way up to us in the sky I couldn't believe it was possible that we would not be hit and shot down. All eight bombs had been released in microseconds but it seemed like all eternity.

The whole manoeuvre lasted a few seconds but time distortion was at work and it seemed as though we were sitting up there for hours. I heard one or two whizzes close to my jet but I saw nothing now that I

PABLO'S WAR

was running away as fast as I could from the target,
at around 600mph. I just wanted to get my little pink
body home as fast as I possibly could.

Thirty seconds later I looked over my right wing
to see number three, Mark Paisey and his navigator
Mike Toft, going as fast and as low as I was. It was
pedal to the metal as we pushed our jets to the limit.
I called my number two, John Peters and John Nicol,
to check that they too were OK and running home
to safety. I got a brief, 'Yes, we are OK, but there
was a problem over the target.' They had missed and
I ordered them to dump their bombs and run south
as fast as they could – it was the quickest way to get
them back over the Saudi border. Then John Nichol
called me again, and this time it was real trouble of the
sort we had all dreaded. Calmly he called, 'Stand by, I
think we have more problems.' His last transmission
came moments later: 'We're on fire, we might have
to get out.'

I knew then that John Peters was fighting to
control the three-quarters that was left of his aircraft.
He had taken a bad hit and had been caught as he
desperately tried to bomb the target. When I listened
to John Nichol's calm words I had no idea if I was
listening to the last words of a dying man. We tried
to call them again but there was no response – they
were gone.

Finally I called again in the hope that they might
hear my last words of advice: 'If you've got to
get out, do it, but leave it as late as you can.' I
wanted them to get to the Saudi border to safety.
The others all quietly listened and we made a mental

note of their approximate position at their last transmission.

We wanted to turn back to help, to do whatever we could to get our two boys home, but it would have been hopeless. There was nothing we could have done to save them and what hit them would be waiting to shoot us down too. But we still wanted to climb just a little higher in the hope that we could spot them, locate where they had crashed or even see signs that they had safely ejected, but our orders were to run and we had to obey.

Even now, when I think about their loss, I still feel the anguish. It was hard to leave them to their fate. What kind of comrades were we to just go? I thought then that if they had died in the cockpit I could never forget it.

As we turned for home I looked over my right shoulder and spotted the white, trailing plume of a SAM (surface-to-air missile). Instantly my attention was focused on this latest deadly danger and I broke hard to the left as it exploded close to my right wing. As soon as we were over the border and into safe airspace Gary transmitted to the American AWACS (airborne warning and control system) and support aircraft that we had lost our wingmen. The Americans responded, as I knew they would. With the slim chance that our crew were still safe and limping home in a damaged jet, any available aircraft they could possibly spare was brought in to scour the region for our lads. But we knew they were already lost as we headed back for mid-air refuelling. The tanker men shared our grief; they had sent three jets safely on their way and only two had returned.

Our two refuelling tankers hung on as long as they dared, draining whatever little was left of their own meagre fuel reserves in the hope that our boys would make it back at least to where they were waiting to help. The tanker crews did more than they were asked, waiting in the air for more than half an hour after we left them, and then flew back into Muharraq on the fumes – that was about all that remained in their own fuel tanks.

Gary and I said nothing to each other as we came in to land, but I know we had both shed a private tear for the men we had lost; there was no room for words. Close to the base I looked across at Mark Paisey, who was flying alongside in perfect formation. I couldn't even tick him off for being out of line, so as to lighten our spirits. The true horror of war had been brought home to us.

That mission had been ninety-eight per cent sheer boredom and two per cent total terror and each mission we flew shared the same routine. But in that two per cent the risks were so great that none of us dared to discuss the possibilities.

Every mission we flew was backed up by incredible American air support. For each Tornado bomber there were six times as many A6 Prowlers and F18 Hornets to soften up defences ahead of the British bombers. On the way back from that first mission we could already see the evidence of the 'Bull's-eye War'. Virtually every bomb dropped had found its intended target. There were many early signs of success as we flew over missile sites and defence systems that were now only vertical plumes of black smoke. Someone had already done their job and they had done it very well.

We flew back to base in silence in the mid-morning sunshine and as we busied ourselves with the routine of flying our aircraft Gary radioed to base that we were coming home without our number two.

As we taxied into our parking slots I could see a crowd of well-wishers who had gathered to welcome us home. While we closed the aircraft down and raised the canopy they could all clearly see that this was not the right time for backslapping praise. We needed to be alone with our thoughts, and slowly they all disappeared, leaving me and Gary sitting together on the tarmac close to our jet.

We dared not say anything to each other, since just one word would have brought an uncontrollable flood of tears. The conflict of emotions was terrible: the sheer exhilaration of coming back and being alive and then the sorrow that we had lost our wingmen, our closest friends. There was still guilt at not having thought of the thing that, so blindingly obviously, would have made their survival chances better. In truth we did all we could for the two Johns but we just didn't feel it was enough.

Almost everyone back at the base shared our terrible grief at their loss and I never once, then or later, felt ashamed or weak about sharing my emotions. Nor do I feel any less of a man because I openly wept at the loss of close friends and comrades, and I resent anyone who believes that this could possibly be a sign of weakness.

I don't really know how long we sat on the tarmac but finally it seemed important to go in and complete the detailed sortie debrief. We handed the jet back to the engineers and walked in silence into the ops building. Every second of our mission was clouded by our loss as I painfully recalled the moment they were shot out of the sky. I was asked to assess their chance of survival. It was like being asked to play God.

I now know much of what happened during those fateful moments up until the two Johns abandoned their stricken jet. In their final approach to the Iraqi airfield their bombs failed to release, which left them still loaded down with four tons of extra weight and helplessly wallowing in mid-air, a sitting target for the enemy to shoot down. At the end of the war their mangled jet was recovered. It had been peppered with 57-mm fire and hit by at least one missile. John Peters later told me that everything behind John Nichol's seat had become a ball of flame, and he was amazed that they had managed to get out alive.

The delight we experienced that they both survived and came home to us after a horrible ordeal in captivity feels good, but I'm not sure if I'll ever be able to talk about their last transmissions again without a lump rising in my throat. I feel the same now as the day it happened, but I'm hoping it will become very much easier for me.

When my formation flew again we would be taking new wingmen and they would already have much to learn. We were veterans now, but so much of what we had learned we could never share with others, for it was our story and ours alone.

We were driven by coach back to our hotel in downtown Bahrain but no one talked and there were no jokes, no laughing, not even tears – we just wanted to get back. My boys should have felt joyous and exhilarated that they had finally proved their mettle but we thought then that our comrades could also be dead.

As we left the base it was obvious that Bahrain was now in a state of war, although we had not seen this when we had left that morning. But now we were coming back to a ghost town, and when we arrived at the hotel we saw that windows had been sealed up to reduce the effects of bomb blast and sandbags were now stacked around the door.

On climbing down from our coach we all stopped and stared hard at a blue Suzuki jeep parked close to the entrance. A British expat who had befriended us had loaned it out to the two Johns for as long as they needed it. No one touched the jeep for days; it just sat there and we hardly dared look at it again as we passed in and out of the hotel.

As we wandered into our hotel I spotted Tony and Beth Robinson, who, only a day before, had fixed our tennis match for that lunchtime. Now I had to apologize to them for losing one of their tennis partners, John Peters. They had sat at our hotel patiently waiting for our return and when they heard my unmistakable grief at the loss of our two comrades they felt the pain as though it was their own. These people shared their lives with us and in doing so they shared our sorrow.

The two Johns had a room in the hotel just a few doors down from the one I shared with Gary, and it was difficult to walk past their door again before a mission or after it. Someone in military administration discreetly packed up their belongings one day while we were out. Weeks later their room was given to another crew, but I never accepted they should be there because to me, until I could share a beer with my lads again, this was still the Johns' room.

Just seventy-two hours after they were shot down we heard our boys were alive. They had been paraded on Iraqi TV and looked horribly bruised and battered, but I was convinced their injuries had been caused by their ejection. Listening to their voices, there was no doubt in my mind that they were already suffering a terrible ordeal. I felt sorry that they would suffer pain and discomfort but I was jubilant that they were alive and would be restored to us as the two Johns we knew. I carried that belief with me for the rest of the war and when we all saw them released I was overjoyed. But I am deeply saddened that now, after all we have shared, it seems we can no longer be friends.

That night, after we came home from our first mission, I felt I had to phone Sheila, because she would have heard the news that we had gone in and she deserved to know that I had come back safely. Our conversation was terribly strained, since I couldn't tell her anything in detail – just that I was alive and that she could sleep easy that night because I wouldn't be flying. The hardest thing for me at first was picking up the telephone, but then it was even harder to end the call, because every time could have been the very last. And it never got easier. Something changed in me and I hope one day I will understand it.

Later that night all that any of us wanted was a beer and a quiet night before bed. We all needed some time alone with our thoughts. We had been issued with something strong to help us sleep, and after war broke out I found I couldn't sleep without it.

Very soon the burden of our loss began to lift. Everything throughout the war was happening at the same lightning pace. It was now time to think ahead. Every time I thought I had reached an emotional frontier something else came along and pushed me through it.

# 2

# Preparation for War

I was blissfully unaware of the significance of 2 August 1990. Early that morning I was driving down from our base at RAF Laarbruch for a long-awaited family holiday: three glorious weeks in the Tuscan hills. I had so looked forward to being with my family away from our forces life, and all we wanted for the next few weeks was each other. Our holiday was going to be great: ten days in a delightful Italian villa high up in the hills where for four miles in every direction we could see nothing but beautiful rolling countryside. Then we were off for another week to a holiday village where our children could have fun making new friends. We had planned the holiday months before, and if it had been delayed by just that one day we wouldn't have gone at all.

For the whole of that year I had been working hard to gain my civilian flying licence and the exams were coming up in November. These were to be my last few months in the RAF and without the prospect of a war I was due to leave at the end of June 1991 in search of an airline pilot's job.

The very first I heard of the Iraqi invasion of

Kuwait was two weeks after it happened, since we had intentionally not even taken a small radio away with us and I was determined not to buy days-old British newspapers. Why should there be anything that could possibly affect our lives?

I was sitting at the pool idly watching my children splash around in the water when a chap staying two apartments away from us came over. He knew from our brief chats together that I was an RAF Tornado pilot and he had already heard BBC reports on his short-wave radio about the Allied build-up in the Gulf and that three Tornadoes had crashed with the loss of five out of six lives after intense training over the North Sea. I believed he assumed I was fully aware of both incidents but his news hit me like a sledgehammer. The peace of that sunny day suddenly disappeared in a haze of uncertainty.

It was not until I got home that I found out I knew all five of the men who had died. I had been up with all three navigators on many occasions and one of them had flown with me, when we had both trained to fly Tornadoes seven years earlier. We had made all our mistakes together in those early days but now he was dead. At the end of a wonderful summer holiday I was faced with the awful realization that those men were almost certainly just the first whose deaths I would have to mourn.

The man who had already fed me enough information to make me realize my holiday was on borrowed time also handed me a five-day-old copy of *The Times* crammed with stories about the brutal invasion, Allied troops on red alert and the British

31

forces preparing for war. Now I needed to know what the hell was really going on and I jumped into our car to drive fifteen miles to the little town of San Gimignano and the nearest public phone to call my squadron back in Germany.

As I drove along on that bright morning I felt intense anxiety about the future. My holiday was wonderful – I was a million miles away from work, from flying fast jets – but I felt a new and terrible gnawing fear of heading into the unknown. I was not put at ease by a senior officer who advised me to return from my holiday in my own time and to relax, since there would be plenty for me to do when I got home. I was frustrated because there had been no reassurance from that telephone call, no one available to explain to me what was going on. They were all too damned busy to worry about soothing my personal anxiety. Half of me wanted to rush back to our apartment, throw a few things into a bag and rush back to base. The rest of me was content to stay with my family and bury my head in the sand.

Years before, as a helicopter pilot serving in Northern Ireland, I had regularly operated from an army base in County Fermanagh, very close to an old Second World War seaplane base. Part of the complex was a maze of underground tunnels dug deep into the hillside. I sometimes dreamt that if ever a nuclear war broke out I would use those hills for my own secret family hideaway. The plan was to collect my family from our home in Hampshire and fly them back in my helicopter with all our belongings so that we could live hidden in those tunnels until it was all over. There was a part of me now that wanted to put that plan into operation.

What disturbed my sleep for the last few nights on holiday was simply not knowing what to expect. For me, this was the feathers-ruffling stage of our preparations for war. For the first time in my eighteen-year career I was going to be allowed to train as I would fight, and it was exciting. This would be the only chance I would ever have in my fast-jet career to show just how good I was at my job.

The first warning I'd been given that I would never have to finally prove myself was when I moved on to Tornado bombers from flying helicopters in the summer of 1982. I was asked by a senior officer, 'How will you handle this: never actually finally carrying out what you've been trained for?'

I'd enjoyed five brilliant years flying RAF helicopters supporting the army in Northern Ireland and on search and rescue missions. And I'd already qualified for 'death-defying' newspaper stories: 'Rotorblades inches from the rock face'; 'Copter crew plucked victim from mountainous waves just inches from the jaws of death'. I'd even had a new-born baby boy named after me when I rushed his grateful mum to hospital in a blizzard. Most of it had been demanding but rewarding, and great fun.

Tornado flying was going to be very different: challenging but with no real professional conclusion, though not without the ultimate challenge of fighting a war. Now we were going to show the world just how well prepared we were to go into this fight. I knew it would smack any aggressor in the face to see how good we were. But all I hoped was that our amazing show of force would persuade Saddam to give up any hope of winning a war. There was never any doubt in my mind that we were going to smash him. To me it always seemed a tragic waste, that we were going to inflict so much suffering and pain to prove what we already knew. Not for a second did I ever doubt our own strength and supremacy.

I am a member of the best team in the world; there is no one anywhere who can touch us. I can state without embarrassment that we are the most select, professional and capable military air-crew anywhere. I don't believe I'm any better than any of those men who went to war with me but I did have that spare capacity needed to lead. Together we made a successful team.

Now the kid gloves of peacetime were off. I was excited and looking forward to training to the limit. My only hope was that any enemy who fought us at our trade had to be insane. Of course that enemy was to be Saddam INSANE!

I'd worked out that at least half the Tornado forces would be sent to the Gulf and the odds were that I would be among them. I had never been to that part of the world before and I was looking forward to training hard and flying hard. Surely the politicians would rattle sabres for long enough for me to get a suntan and come home. That belief sustained me right up until the day I flew into war.

The odds were unthinkable: to me it was like a football team of schoolboys challenging Liverpool or me offering to fight Mike Tyson. I saw it as half a million Boy Scouts against a crack team of half a million SAS men. The outcome didn't bear thinking about: there would be carnage and we would be inflicting the damage. I totally discounted the prospect of going to war.

I came home from holiday to a war effort and flew intensely from then on. The guys who were already at work had been in the frame for three weeks. I was relaxed and at ease while many of my pals had already lived through a full-scale alert. For the first few weeks back at base it was a stop-start situation. We were given top priority for training and told we would be the first aircrew deployed to the Gulf. Within days those instructions were revised; other squadrons would leave ahead of us. Some days we were going to spearhead the entire operation, on other days we would stay at home while other Tornado bases led the way.

I said goodbye to my family three times. We had my departure all planned. There would be no tearful goodbyes at the front door of our home, no last words to Michael and Ellie that might become a sad epitaph to our parting. I did not want my children to be aware that there was a possibility that I would never see them again. I wanted to make it easy for all of us but most of all I didn't want them to remember the departure. I wanted them only to remember the good times and have nothing but happy memories of us being together. It seemed enough that if the very worst did happen then all they needed to know was that Daddy left for work one afternoon and never came home.

Leaving my family was always going to be difficult for me and for my wife Sheila even though we had talked about our parting many times. At best it was going to be the longest single time away from my family, while at worst it would be the last time I ever saw them.

A week before I left for the Gulf we invited all seven boys from my team, with their wives and girlfriends, to the house for a final marvellous thrash. No house rules were laid down; no topics of conversation were taboo. Everyone was actually aware of what had brought us together and the reason why we were there. There was a distinct possibility that at some time in the future some of those young wives sitting around our dinner table would become young widows. For that night at least, and well into the early hours of the next morning, we had a wonderful time.

After we had finished our meal I stood and offered a simple toast that one day, when all this stupidity was over, we would all sit around this table again. After I came home from war it just never seemed the right thing to do – it was enough for me to know that everyone who had been present that night was available to be there again.

Laarbruch was frantic with activity, with its maintenance areas where night was turned into day by powerful floodlights so that the ground crews could work round the clock preparing our jets for the desert. You could hear the constant hum of high-powered compressors and generators several miles from the base. This constant background noise was regularly punctuated by the powerful roar of a jet engine being brought to life on its test bed.

Almost everyone was working with a new sense of purpose, for this was not a realistic exercise – it was preparation for war. Helmet visors had an extra gleam and aircraft canopies shone like never before. Efficiency in the service that I loved and that had been my whole life for so many years had always been good but now it reached new levels, much higher than I had ever known.

Those who failed to recognize that every single one of us was part of this massive effort were quickly brought into line. It was late one evening when a two-man flying crew returned to the officers' mess where they ate and slept, having finally achieved a successful training mission. They had been at work for twenty solid hours, which far exceeded any peacetime duty limits, and they had been frustrated by aircraft problems and operational restrictions over Germany. Finally, they were ready for a hot meal and a hot bath before bed, only to discover that dinner had been over a good twenty minutes and the best that the kitchen staff could offer was a sandwich. It was the final straw and the guys just blew a fuse. The mess manager was summoned and juicy steaks, fresh vegetables and enough to feed half a dozen crews miraculously arrived on the table. Hot meals, day or night, were never a problem again.

A lot of events at my base had been brought

forward that year, including the annual children's
Christmas party now scheduled for 2 December. It
was perfect timing, for only two weeks earlier orders
for me to fly to the Gulf had been given and I had
pencilled that same date into my personal diary. This
was where all the planning Sheila and I had discussed
so many times would take over: she would take the
kids to their party at lunchtime and I would leave
our home near the base a couple of hours later. It
seemed easier that way. I could never have predicted
what was later to happen minutes before I boarded
the bus to take me to a waiting Hercules transport
aircraft fifty miles away at RAF Wildenrath.

I hadn't said a last word to Sheila or the kids
as we parted, but simply stood at the end of our
path and waved as they drove away to their party.
After so many years together all that Sheila needed
to say to me was, 'Come back.' I needed those next
precious moments alone to take a last look at each of
the children's bedrooms and a final look at the room
I shared with my wife. The bed had been made but
I could still see the soft hollows where two heads
had rested on two pillows. Would I ever be sleeping
there again?

Three of us were to drive to the base together: my
navigator, Gary Stapleton, was going to collect me in
his family's second car before we picked up another
colleague, Mike Toft. When Gary pulled up I was
already waiting outside. No one said a word as we
drove into the base; each of us stared hard out of
his own window. It was still all going to plan as I
walked out of the armoury where I had been handed

my personal weapon. Then, on my way back to the squadron, I walked straight into Ellie and Mike.

It was like being given some massive jolt, bringing me back to earth with a crash landing, as I suddenly realized just what I would be leaving behind. I saw my kids full of the joys of their party and it hit me right in the heart. I had got through my private contemplation at home all right, tidying away my thoughts and feelings along with my overnight bag; I had felt so strong then but this was more than I could possibly bear. I couldn't speak – the words were buried somewhere deep inside me as I held both children very tight in my arms. Then at last I let them go and turned to walk away; I couldn't let them see my face.

I clambered on to the waiting bus already crammed with our overnight bags, essential kit and the last-minute additions that none of us could possibly do without yet had almost forgotten to pack. I felt strange, for clearly not everyone was sombre at our departure. It was like some weird carnival celebration, as though we were off to have a good time, as some guys hugged and kissed their wives and each other's wives. I couldn't share their joy but I wanted to be happy for them. Were they masking their true feelings or had they simply been carried away on the tide of this international rescue mission on which we were about to embark?

I had done my best early that very morning to talk to Mike about my going to war. I just told him that although mummy was much older, he was now the man of the house and it was his job to take care of her and Ellie until I came home. I was very proud of him then, as I am now. He was ten years old, and I came home to see my child had grown into a young man. Like all kids, he has an amazing resilience and still has that same impish excitement about fast jets and all the other machines of war. But he also understood that I was going off to danger.

Even Ellie, at only eight, knew I was going and why, since she had sat through many of the conversations I'd had with Sheila about future possibilities. Like many of the other men, I'd managed to increase my life insurance. In the past I had taken care of everything for my family but if I didn't come back I wanted it all to be made easy for Sheila. We made all the practical arrangements together and did our best to sit on our emotions. As the time came closer to going, it really didn't take a rocket scientist to work out that if there was going to be a war I'd be slap-bang in the middle of it.

Christmas also came early for many of the other guys that year, but I decided that I wouldn't buy any presents and I didn't – at least not until the war was over. When I came home at the end of March I was weighed down with gifts, including a solid-gold bangle for Sheila, a gold necklace for Ellie and a yachtsman's watch for Mike. I looked hard at the aviator's watch but decided it really didn't have enough dials and knobs for a young lad of ten.

Some guys sent Christmas presents home, while others took gift-wrapped presents from their families out to the Gulf. Sheila and the kids sent out a card and a little teddy bear, but they knew there would be no Christmas parcel from me in return. I didn't want some memorial sitting on the mantelpiece. I preferred my family to remember the happiness we had shared together.

I arrived in the Gulf after twenty-four hours aboard the Hercules, suffering the wearying effects of travelling in an aircraft designed for transporting packing boxes, not people. It was always either too hot or so cold you could see the ice forming on the inside of the windows. There was no room to stretch out to snatch a few moments' sleep, so packed was it with tools and personnel of war.

Some of the boys came prepared for boredom with magnetic chess sets or cards. I loved a game of cards; one moment we'd be halfway through a round of bridge and the next the plane would hit an air pocket, flinging us and the cards everywhere. The next half hour was always spent scrabbling about after stray cards and arguing about the hand you had just lost and would have surely won with.

We landed at Muharraq airbase on Bahrain, descending from a beautifully clear sky into brilliant noon sunshine. The place was already a hive of activity; it seemed that any piece of desert within the airfield perimeter that was not already concrete was shortly to become so. There were diggers, bulldozers and cement-mixers everywhere. Someone was making a lot of money. Anywhere already converted to concrete had quickly been claimed and was piled high with bombs, ammunition, ration packs and an assortment of crash-recovery vehicles.

41

I was welcomed by an old friend, Steve Randles, who looked fit and suntanned and at least a stone and a half heavier than I ever remembered him and than his wife, Jacqui, would allow him to be when he got home. He was glowing with health, and it made him seem so experienced and full of confidence in his sand-coloured desert flying suit. By contrast, I was still pink and naïve in my green flying suit. Then he gave me a hug, almost a bear hug. It was great to see a genuinely friendly face amid all that commotion and uncertainty.

The aircraft pans were stacked with jets of every description. There was a strange mix; here was a military organization still trying to operate as an international airport, but Heathrow – the busiest airport in the world – had seen nothing like this intensity. We were thrown into action as soon as we arrived; issued with even more anti-chemical kit and handed our flying programme for the next day.

We had just spent twenty-four hours travelling hard, with no chance to sleep or even rest. Having left our base on a cool northern European autumn afternoon, we were now standing under the full blaze of a Middle Eastern desert sun.

The squadron boss insisted that we were making our final preparations for war and therefore we would start our desert training the following day. He was apparently quite prepared to risk sending jet-lagged crews into the air. I informed him, as politely as I possibly could, that I would be totally and utterly dejected if Saddam and his boys managed to kill any of my boys, but I was buggered if I was going to do it first!

This was only the first of many occasions when I believed I had to flex my muscles in the interest of my team. I hoped that every other formation leader felt the same way about the men under their command. There are many ways to skin a cat and I had already decided that I was going to use my own tried-and-tested method.

After a day's rest we began our desert training in earnest, right in the heart of the Gulf theatre of operations. Almost every day we flew two-hour training sorties in conditions that none of us had ever experienced before. Even desert-survival training had long been abandoned by the RAF. We had a lot to learn and the best guess around was that we probably had just six weeks to get it right.

There was a constant debate about the need to train as we meant to fight the war, but the rules were to remain, and we were ordered by a senior commander not to fly below 100ft. Of course, I briefed my aircrew accordingly, but I also told them I was determined that anything we could do in training that we would be called upon to do in war, we would go right ahead and do.

I know that most other formations were flying with exactly the same attitude as my team, yet whenever I tried to bring the subject up at executive meetings it was always put on the back burner. We all knew what we were doing but there seemed to be no need to bother higher authority with requests for permission to do it legally. No one would stand up and be counted, yet we were all flying at heights well below 100ft.

There were no trees, so we flew at camel-top height. Yet the rules were that we were forbidden to fly below 100ft. It was so damn frustrating. How on earth could we flagrantly disobey some rules and still expect our boys to respect any of the other rules?

On Christmas Eve we were given a rare opportunity to fly north from Bahrain; no closer than fifty miles to the Saudi border but close enough to see what the ground troops were up to. I didn't believe what I was seeing: along a main supply route to the front we overflew a military convoy travelling nose to tail with heavy lorries, armoured cars, tank transporters and personnel carriers. As we approached the head of the convoy the line of vehicles rumbling along below us towards the front line simply vanished into a sea of dust. We overflew the tail end of that convoy ten minutes later. That one single line of military might was over sixty miles long.

We overflew countless supply depots, each one a mighty military arsenal. Trying to describe those preparations we could see on the ground was almost impossible. I had expected to see a massive military build-up but when I encountered what was actually there it came as an incredible shock. There was a tremendous surge of pride in being a part of this build-up but it was tinged with disbelief; I actually felt scared by the sheer size of it all and I was fighting on the same side.

At ultra-low level we flew our planned war tactics.

Anything that looked remotely inhabited or military we avoided as soon as we picked it up on radar or one of my eagle-eyed youngsters had called it out to the rest of the formation. With our essential training complete and our position about sixty miles south of the Kuwaiti border, it was time to relax a little and head for home. I eased up to 1000ft and, for a challenge, I called my team into a tight box formation, which looks pretty but has no earthly purpose in war. I slowed down to 360mph and we headed south back to Muharraq.

As we flew home I kept calling to my boys to ease backwards and forwards or left to right, to maintain that perfect box shape. Sometimes the movement would need a change of only a couple of feet in any direction. When we finally landed back at base a few of the guys wanted to know how I had ever managed to monitor every aircraft's position at the same time, even the aircraft directly behind me. One asked, 'Do you really have eyes in the back of your head?' I gave them a wry smile, for in truth I had kept them in shape by watching their shadows move on the flat desert floor, but they didn't need to know that.

From the day we began our preparations for war the learning curve for all of us had been vertical. There were many days, right back to the moment I returned from holiday, when I would learn some new skill or technique. The next day I would be teaching it to some of the younger guys on the squadron.

On the night of 21 August I flew my first-ever night air-to-air refuelling sortie, one of the most diffi-cult and demanding pure flying skills that a Tornado

45

pilot is ever required to perform. An experienced pilot, Dave Beveridge, from RAF Marham back in the UK, had come out to Germany especially to give me the benefit of his experience. Normally, to achieve expertise at this would take several sorties of intensive training. To teach this skill to another flyer should take months, if not a year, of practice.

Seven nights later, on my third-ever night refuelling, there I was sitting in the inky-black night in the back seat of another Tornado, trying to teach the pilot the secrets of a skilful refuel. He coped superbly, despite my far from gifted instruction.

To me, although I'd been back at work just a few hours, there was no time to ease gently back into the swing of life. Here I was, already attempting to jump on to a roller-coaster that had been careering along gathering momentum for three weeks. I had no choice other than to close my eyes and jump aboard or fall by the wayside. I jumped for it and I managed to hang on. This particular ride was always guaranteed to come up with some new and exciting twist, especially when I was least expecting it.

In the twelve days that remained of August I could normally have expected to fly just ten hours. In fact I flew almost thirty. This, more than double the average rate, would continue for the next six months. One of my concerns in my preparation for civilian flying was whether or not I would manage to notch up the required five hours of night flying in the remaining months of my active service career. Only eight days after returning from my holiday I had flown well over five hours in darkness.

Towards the end of the month we were flying regular sorties against UK-based fighters. They were preparing for the same war as us and once in the Gulf we would be on the same side, but over the countryside of the north of England they were Iraqi fighters that we were desperate to evade and we were enemy bombers they were intent on shooting down. The debrief after every one of these sorties lasted longer than the sortie itself. Each of us was determined to learn every possible lesson that could be learnt about avoiding enemy aircraft while we were still all firing blanks.

I won't deny I found the going tough for much of the time. We were working incredibly long hours, cramming everything we could think of into our working day. The routine was always the same, since we trained away from home as well as at our own base. We would get up, have breakfast, arrive for our brief, fly and then debrief before a couple of beers and bed. It was always a fourteen-hour day, but it was exciting. Whenever I had an hour to spare, out came my navigation and air-law books to help me through my exams for the civilian licence, which I was determined to pass. It seemed ironic that I was trying hard to revise my knowledge of air law and all its rules in my spare time when professionally I was doing everything imaginable to break them.

Despite the prospect of war, my boss still encouraged me to work hard in preparation for the time when I would be looking for a pilot's job outside the RAF. I was given time off for all the studying I needed and to take exams in Bournemouth. But despite all this I was still on call and could be whisked back to base at a moment's notice.

By the end of September we were flying regular training missions out of RAF Leuchars in Scotland, and by now my overnight bag was getting a regular bashing. Sheila and the kids had come to expect me when they saw me and the odd night away didn't seem to matter; it had become an ever-increasing part of the routine.

At this stage we still had no definite deployment date for the Gulf, but we were assured it was still weeks away. Rather than a planned and orderly movement of our air forces to the Gulf it seemed that the top brass were waiting for the next crisis to happen so that they could then manage it. Some days we would arrive at work to be told that we were under twelve hours' notice to move, and on others we were told to relax as we would not be needed for at least a month.

After several false alarms I decided to close my eyes and ears to anything but the facts. If it wasn't actually happening to me I would simply assume it wasn't going to. Despite this the top brass still managed to swing a few surprises on me and my men. After one night sortie the boss was summoned to receive an urgent phone call immediately after our arrival at Leuchars. Up until now we had been told to continue our routine training – that was, until the boss returned ashen-faced from the phone. There was nothing to discuss; he simply issued the new orders. We would return to Germany the next morning and in twelve hours we would be back in the UK for a further month's intensive training, and then on to the Gulf. Everything I had planned for the next four weeks would now be crammed into just twelve hours.

I telephoned Sheila with the news. We were both tense and I could sense she was trying as hard as I was not to sound upset. We agreed that she would keep the kids off school the next day and we would find somewhere nice for a family trip together. But by the time I got back to Laarbruch the next morning the crisis was over and we carried on with our training. At least my kids enjoyed their day off school.

Training gathered pace with every day and every mission. For the first time in my career I was doing everything with my jet that a Tornado could possibly do and there were none of the peacetime restrictions imposed to minimize the loss of life. Survival chances were always assessed in terms of what is an acceptable risk to life and limb, and if this risk had perhaps been quantified as one in a hundred, it had now come down to one in ten. For me this chance was proven by the tragically higher loss of aircraft and crew in the build-up to war than in the war itself.

We were training seven days a week, with only the odd day off to be with our families, but it was fantastic. By November we had all the facilities for flying missions we had only ever dreamt of in the past. Airspace for flying, tankers for mid-air refuelling, airfields to simulate attacks and ranges to practise our weapons firing were made available any time we needed them; it was unheard of.

Just before I finally flew out to the Gulf I discovered with great amusement that the medical centre at Laarbruch had, rather embarrassingly, run out of condoms. All the aircrews could have explained precisely why, and the medical officer in charge need only have wandered around some of our firing ranges to find out what had happened. We had used them to practise firing our handguns after the range sergeant had discovered they made perfect targets blown up and painted with Saddam Hussein's face – the ranges were littered with them!

We were putting the razor edge on our training, but just before my last sortie before flying out to the Gulf I came very close to becoming another pre-war training statistic. I had been pushing my team to their limits, since there had been too many instances where a poorly chosen line of advance through a valley or over a hilltop had made one of my team vulnerable, perhaps only for a few seconds, but that was enough in war to get him shot down and to expose the rest of us to danger.

At high level over the North Sea on our way back to Germany I casually looked out at an airliner passing overhead and was shocked to see that my port navigation light was smashed. I called my wingman John Peters to take a look from his jet; it was obvious I had hit something solid.

My brush with death made all the papers. I had hit some power cables in Scotland and they were not the sort strung from 200-ft pylons. They were later assessed as having been around 60ft above the ground. I should like to thank the helicopter pilot who got me out of serious trouble when he made that very generous assessment. We had plunged a village into darkness and if I had been a couple of feet lower I would have also crashed a Tornado jet into the Scottish countryside. I had been stupid, since no one was shooting at me, and I later realized I had just been trying too hard. This time I had been very lucky and I just prayed that my luck would continue to hold out. If someone had issued me with nine lives I had just needlessly wasted one of them.

Within a week I had been given a dressing-down by the Deputy Commander in Chief RAF Germany and he really meant it. But, despite his obvious anger, his last words as he put his arm around me were: 'Good luck.' Two days later I finally left for the Gulf.

I was determined to ignore Christmas that year and we had already decided to put our New Year's celebrations on ice. My life was being held on the pause button and I kept it there until the day I came home from war.

Some of our real desert training sorties were the most thrilling moments of flying I had ever known. At times I was nervous about my own ability but I was also more excited than I could ever remember. Flying so fast and low over a featureless desert, I felt I could see for ten million miles. For at the moment I was safe, and relying on my own capabilities was enough to guarantee my return. But at war, in that visibility and with nowhere to hide, I would be like a sitting duck.

We flew regularly with a full war load of fuel and

bombs. At a total weight of well over twenty-eight tons – our peacetime maximum load – our agile Tornadoes were transformed into something more like an aerodynamic house brick, but they were still flyable. For unbelievable exhilaration I can never forget taking a team of eight jets in a tight 'V' formation for a trip down 'Star Wars Valley' in the Saudi Arabian mountains close to the eastern shores of the Red Sea.

We had already heard other guys talking about the thrills of fast flying through these mountains and we were all dying to have a go. The valley started out flat with a wide sandy floor about three miles wide. On each side the mountains rose vertically with towering red rock up to 3000ft high punctuated by narrow red pillars. It was like a Scalextric track, only we were racing with fast jets instead of toy cars.

I could get the whole formation into the wide valley until gradually the floor narrowed to a very sharp 'V' before the valley opened up again. I had never known flying like this, and an eighty-minute sortie seemed like an orgasm lasting several minutes. After we got back to base no one needed to use their aircraft steps – we were all walking 10ft tall.

Another fine sortie took us to the eastern side of friendly Oman on New Year's Eve. I had been flying with my navigator, Gary, for several weeks now and I knew he trusted me, but I decided to put ourselves and the pilot John Peters and his navigator, John Nichol, to the test. We flew off to discover an amazing valley which spread out to a wide bowl at the bottom and climbed to 2500-ft-high peaks at each side. I led with my jet flying as fast as I could up to the top before pulling a roll to fly down to the very bottom of the bowl and then screaming right up and out again. There was silence on the radio as we came out, then very quietly Gary said, 'If you ever do that to me again, teddy will be thrown right out of the cot and I won't eat my tea!' I think he may have found our trip a little too exhilarating.

I came home to base after a two-hour sortie and we were running frighteningly low on fuel. There had been no Victor tanker available for mid-air refuelling, and I was flying in on what was left in my tanks. As I came in to the final stages of my approach there was a gas attack called on the airfield. I knew then there would be no chance of being allowed to land.

There were two jets left up in the air – myself flying with Gary and John Peters with John Nichol. The only option left to us was to scurry as fast as we dare allow ourselves to Sheik Isa, an American airbase down the road. But as I approached to land again, I, in my front seat, suffered a total radio failure at precisely the moment my engines decided to play up. Gary could still talk to John Peters, who was leading us in to land, but it was getting desperate and I screamed to Gary at the top of my voice that if the runway was not cleared for us within two minutes we would be planting our Tornado in the sand about two miles short, since I had run out of fuel and ideas.

We came in on the fumes – I had never seen my fuel gauges so low – and we sat on the tarmac for some time, simply relieved at being there. As I closed down the aircraft I stopped and looked around at the place where we had landed. I had never seen so much military hardware in my life; it was an incredible sight. Every single square foot of concrete had aircraft sitting on it. There were small fighter jets parked under bigger ones and they were all tightly crammed alongside huge bombers and transporters. There was simply no space left to take any more aircraft and the Americans were not too happy with the prospect of having to find somewhere for our Tornadoes.

The American duty officer from the base came out to meet us and I apologized to him for dropping in unannounced, but I had had no alternative to landing at Sheik Isa other than to eject. In absolute seriousness he requested that I should consider that alternative in future, since there was simply nowhere for us to park. We refuelled quickly and left.

All that I could think before we left, as I looked around at this vision of Allied might, was just who the hell would be crazy enough to take us on?

# 3

# Why Am I Here?

For as long as I can remember, I have been a bit of a chameleon. I'm able to adapt fully to my surroundings and, in most cases, take the best possible advantage of whatever conditions I may be faced with.

As a military man, I've endured conditions that an outsider would undoubtedly describe as squalid. On several exercises over the years, I have lived under a hedgerow and survived on grubs, berries or fish poached out of streams well out of season. I have also feasted on small wild animals which were unlucky enough to become ensnared in my makeshift traps. In Northern Ireland, on helicopter squadrons, I enjoyed far from palatial surroundings. In South Armagh I lived behind barbed wire, sandbags and concrete.

But I have also enjoyed absolute luxury when I have taken part in air displays, and in public and private events where the aircrews were accommodated in first-class hotels.

In the Gulf War, too, I was one of the lucky ones. I fought my war from a five-star hotel. The high-rise

Sheraton Hotel in Bahrain was a far cry from much of the make and mend that was going on at our airbase just a few miles away on the island of Muharraq.

My home for the past seven years had been West Germany, but for the next four months it would be Bahrain. They are separated by a distance of only 3000 miles – a relatively short distance today – but in cultural terms it could have been different planets.

It seemed to me, from my very early impressions of this dusty, bustling city, that most of the Bahrainis followed exactly the same lifestyle as their forefathers had done for generations. But there were many glaring contradictions to this historic, deeply religious way of life. On the horizon you could see a towering block of luxury apartments or a plush hotel, with a glitz and glitter that made them seem as though they had just been transported from downtown Las Vegas and planted in the desert. Yet in the shadows of these massive Western constructions there would be half a dozen dhows, ancient Arab sailing vessels with their single masts, sitting on the mud-flats waiting for the tide to come in. Then their occupants would go about their fishing or smuggling, which I was to discover is a popular local industry.

It was intriguing just to sit and watch, or photograph, these extraordinary people simply going about their daily lives, wearing a style of clothes that had not changed in centuries. Their wooden sailing ships, once used by the slave traders in East Africa, had also never changed, either in design or method of construction, for hundreds of years.

Among all this ancient culture, a tremendous

Western influence had taken root. But there is a point at which the Arabs' way of life firmly forbids any further incursion by Western ideology.

We had been fully briefed about Bahrain's culture and the need of its people to pray five times a day. We had been advised to show respect to the people and their Islamic faith.

One day soon after my arrival in Bahrain, I went out on one of many shopping trips around the dark and narrow maze of paths that led around the Souk, the bustling Arab market. At one of countless fabulous carpet shops, I paused to admire the fine Persian, Chinese and Indian rugs on display. The proud owner greeted me with open arms. I was the customer he had been waiting all day to meet. We enjoyed a glass of sweet mint tea together, discussed the many problems of the world and how the desert map could be redrawn as a result of the threatened war in the Middle East.

I had taken a fancy to one of his many fine carpets. We bargained, and he told me his best possible price. Here was a rug that he very much wanted me to have. He could tell I was a genuine person who would look after this rug and cherish it as he would himself. Of course, he would make no living out of this rug because I drove such a hard bargain. I wondered how many times in the past this same story had been told, but it was enormous fun.

Suddenly I heard a little bell ringing outside. It made no difference to my continuing interest in my first taste of Arabic bartering. But the shopkeeper promptly ended our negotiations by saying, 'I am sorry, Sir. Now I must pray.' He turned away from me in mid sentence to pull a small silk rug from a drawer, knelt down on it and cupped his hands into his face as he began to pray to his God.

I tried not to focus on this very private communication with Allah. But I was almost like a fly on the wall, witnessing some very personal activity that I had no part in. I felt distinctly uncomfortable in the few minutes that he knelt and prayed, moving his head back and forth to the floor, uttering his incomprehensible incantations. But he apparently felt no discomfort at my presence.

After the prayers came to an end, he raised himself from the floor, bowed and rolled his rug away. Then he joined me to continue the conversation that had been so abruptly suspended minutes before.

In those few minutes of time, he had vanished into his religion. It was a cultural void that I do not believe the West can ever hope to cross.

I later discovered many more examples of this divide, even among Bahraini businessmen who dealt daily with Western banks, construction companies and manufacturers. I could understand the glaring differences between ourselves and the desert Arabs who rarely made the journey into town. But many of these Bahrainis dressed in smart French designer suits and dined at all the best Western-style hotels and restaurants. It was their faith, that unbending, uncompromising allegiance to Allah, that ultimately made their private way of life appear worlds apart from our own.

One of the things that most struck me about the

place was that it seemed hypocritical that Bahrain should share a common causeway linking it to Saudi Arabia. There was Saudi, a dry country where alcohol is abhorred as the Devil's own juices. Its use is absolutely against the law and Saudis who have been found to have drunk alcohol have had their fingers or even hands removed. Yet throughout my time in Bahrain the bars in many hotels, and the bars downtown, were invariably packed with Saudis getting drunk on alcohol. I could not understand this double standard. Perhaps they would return across that causeway the following day, having shaken off a shocking hangover, to once again extol the virtues of an alcohol-free existence.

Those Saudis I met during my time in Bahrain were as capable of tying one on as famed drinking nations like we Brits, the Germans or the Australians.

Bahrain is an island of contradictions. You can look in almost any direction and see a breathtaking display of immense wealth. You would see a huge palace, a gold-plated Rolls-Royce or a Bahraini dripping with gold jewels. Change direction again and there would be an example of abject poverty: a Bahraini in rags, living in a squalid roadside hut.

But the owners of fabulous luxury cars or splendid homes never had to fear that their vehicles would be stolen or their homes plundered. Crime on the island is virtually non-existent and it took me some time when I finally returned home to remember to lock the car door. In Bahrain I could leave a car anywhere and not even bother to remove the keys.

Crime is summarily dealt with by the ruling

family. During the early days of our stay, an American serviceman was stabbed by a Bahraini. It turned out that his attacker was suffering from a mental disorder; he was not a thug or a villain. But the ruler of Bahrain, Sheik Eissa bin Sulman Al-Khalifa, decreed that such an incident would never happen again. No statement was issued by the local police or the politicians. A simple edict was made by the ruler of these people that there would be no more incidents of this nature. Nothing like that ever did happen to any of us again. I could go wherever I wanted, whenever I wanted, in total safety.

Once inside the Sheraton Hotel, which was to be my home for the duration of the Gulf War, I could have mentally transported myself to any major capital city in the world. It was a luxury hotel with only a few clues as to its location, such as the gold-plated signs in Arabic over the restaurants and bars.

Gary and I found ourselves sharing a room on the first of fifteen floors. Formerly single-person accommodation, it had been hastily adapted to provide homes for the two-man aircrews. There were two divan-sized beds, one pushed up against a wall by the window, which I chose.

We had our own marble bathroom stocked with expensive hair shampoos, body lotions and soaps for the overnight traveller. Often, we would play a game with the staff, whose job it was to ensure our bathrooms were kept constantly supplied with fresh towels and an array of toiletries.

We would remove the top from a bottle of after-shave or bath oil, and pour just a little out before replacing the top. Sure enough, when the room had been valeted by one of the Indian servants, those containers would all have been thrown out and replaced.

I found it so frustrating that I could never get to use a bar of soap for more than one day. I'd wash my face once, scarcely taking the engraved initials of the Sheraton Hotel off the ivory bar. The next time I returned to our room, there would be a virgin bar of soap. I have never been used to this kind of waste and I felt like hiding my bar of soap so that I would be allowed to use it all up.

Yet it was amazing how quickly we all adapted to our new, luxury lifestyle. Gary preferred his shirts starched and returned on a hanger. I liked mine folded and they would be returned to our room in a sealed bag.

That laundry bill alone must have cost someone in the treasury a small fortune. You could buy a packet of handkerchiefs down in the Bahraini market for about £2. But we couldn't get an allowance for handkerchiefs so we sent our used ones off to the hotel laundry. I discovered that the cost of laundering just two ordinary handkerchiefs was actually £2.

We enjoyed all the trappings of luxury, such as a huge TV and a refrigerator stocked with drinks ranging from a couple of beers to a quarter bottle of champagne. But I do not feel any guilt at having enjoyed that luxury just because many others were forced to endure far poorer conditions throughout the war. We had the best possible accommodation of all the forces. Yet many of our allies who experienced that luxury for a weekend away from the desert, or a couple of days snatched from living beside a tank, or under a truck, told us that they would not have changed places with us for a king's ransom. For them, it took away the absolute concentration that they felt would be required for them to commit themselves to a war.

There was not one Tornado operator that I spoke to, either during or after the war, who was envious of our comforts at Bahrain. They were based at other locations, either in the desert or in Dahran. The quality of their leisure time was probably considerably poorer than mine but they would not have changed places with me. I certainly had no desire to change places with them.

I could imagine that the soldier who was living in the desert, or the sailor who was locked in the bowels of his ship, for months on end, might have wanted to change their lifestyles with us so that we could see what life was really like down at the rough end. But would they have swapped their military roles with us too? I defy anyone who was out in the Gulf and not flying Tornado ground-attack aircraft day after day, to say he would have willingly taken my seat.

For me, life in Bahrain would have been far from complete without the tremendous contribution that was made to the quality of our lives by the British expatriate community living there. It seemed that from almost the moment we arrived, they couldn't do enough to make us feel welcome. They never hesitated in telling us that they felt eternally grateful for the job we were out there to do. In many ways, they lived their lives around us for the duration of our stay.

Up until the outbreak of war there were numerous house parties, which were inevitably wild affairs. If, for any reason, a group of us was unable to accept an invitation because of flying training or another commitment, the hosts would always change the date to ensure our presence. During the war, it was always open house. They would welcome us into their homes at any time of the night or day. We could sit alone there, read a book, watch TV or simply chat. All they wanted to do was to give and they expected nothing in return. The debt of gratitude I still feel towards the expats is one that I don't believe I shall ever be able to repay.

John and Nuala Wright became my very special friends outside of RAF life. John had been a squadron leader education officer in the RAF, but his job in Bahrain was to represent the British Council. It is hard for me to describe in a few words the very special relationship I had with John. He knew exactly how to listen, when to say something and when to say nothing. I could have written down all the pearls of wisdom that he offered me during those terrible days of war, and many more since. They would have been of great benefit to many others in need of support and understanding. To me, John was a sage.

I first met John and Nuala at the Hash House

Restaurant, a delightful little eating house just off the Al Fateh highway, behind the Gulf Hotel. John was dining at a table with friends and I had taken my boys along on spec. He asked us to share his wine and very soon we had struck up a conversation.

After our meal he invited us back to his wonderful house. Straight out of the British Raj, it was a rectangular building with a flat roof, and each floor had its own verandah encircling the house. Large columns and parapets, many of them in disrepair, were now undergoing the tender ministrations of John to bring the house back to its former glory.

The house stood in two acres of palm trees and was surrounded by high, dark-green hedges and perfectly manicured lawns. At one end of the grounds was a grand gated entrance, outside which a Bahraini policeman kept guard. The whole atmosphere of the place was redolent of the end of the British Empire. John and Nuala had furnished their palatial home to perfection. I went there often, when no one else was at home, just to sit in the grounds and be alone. It became a retreat that was generously made available to all of us whenever we wanted it.

The kindness of people like John and Nuala, and many others of the expat community, was particularly important to me, because I had not been in Bahrain long when I found myself in a moral dilemma. For I realized that I had little respect for the people we were fighting for. It also quickly became clear that they had no respect for us and, shockingly, they also seemed to care very little even for each other.

One terrible night I shall never forget. The Iraqis had begun attacking Allied airbases with Scud missiles and just after midnight the air-raid sirens began to wail. For a few minutes I remained in my bed, half dozing, as I tried to forget the stark images rushing through my mind of a daylight bombing raid over Baghdad.

This was to be my first and only visit to the safety of the makeshift bunker in the basement of the Sheraton Hotel. After what later happened there I vowed never to go again. It was easier to disobey direct orders and take my chances in the solitude of my first-floor hotel room with the comfort of a bottle of five-star brandy.

I shall never forget how embarrassed I felt at arriving down in the bowels of the hotel among the heating pipes and dusty storerooms, equipped with my full service-issue chemical warfare suit and gas mask, only to find that many of the civilians who had hurried there for safety – mostly Kuwaiti refugees – had no more than a damp cloth to hold over their faces for protection against a gas attack.

They were already huddled together on the cold, bare floor, wild-eyed and apprehensive about what new terror the next few moments may bring. A terrified Kuwaiti woman, clutching a child about the same age as my own daughter, Ellie, looked hopefully at me as though she believed I could offer her some help. I had orders to wear my gas mask whenever an air-raid alert had been sounded. But just looking at the frightened sea of faces of this pitiful little bunch of homeless people made it unbearable for me to sit there alongside them in my gas mask.

I simply could not stand the thought of sitting there breathing in safe air while facing the awful prospect of watching all those helpless and defence-less people slowly choke to death around me. If the Iraqis had realized all our worst nightmares by launching a chemical attack, these innocent and now stateless civilians around me would have suffered a horribly painful death.

I tore off my mask and tightened the straps so they would fit around the little girl's head. But when I tried to help her on with my mask, her mother snatched it from my hands and held it tightly to her own face. I stood there, completely speechless for just a moment, and then moved back to my own space on the floor in disbelief.

During the very early stages of the conflict, I honestly believe that I did not even ask myself why I was there at all. It probably did not matter then, while we were all totally absorbed with the job we had to do and with preserving our own little pink bodies. But it did not take long for me to become fairly convinced that I was fighting somebody else's war. This was certainly not a war that I was responsible for. I had trained hard during my entire military career for a probable, and then as the years went by, an increasingly unlikely war in Europe which would, if it occurred, be against the Russians.

Whenever we carried out a training exercise to prepare us for this conflict we used coloured marker boards to denote our plans of attack or defence. We, the good guys, and our allies, with all our vast combined armies, airforces and navies, were always the blue forces. The mighty Russian bear that had so wanted to rule the world became the orange forces. It was always blue versus orange.

On the rare occasions when I had paused to consider what I was doing and why, I could always rationalize my role in our armed forces. It always made sense to me that we needed to maintain a military presence in Europe so that the shopkeepers could go about their shopkeeping and the school-teachers could carry on teaching future generations of our children. The low-flying complainers could also carry on protesting about our fast jets on essential low-level training exercises.

Everything always had a reason, which made my job both worthwhile and fundamentally essential: to keep the free world safe from communism and all its ensuing evils. It also became clear then that the enemy I had always prepared for and its military might was there in spite of the people rather than to support them. By contrast, I never had any doubt that I was there to support my fellow countrymen and defend their freedom. Maybe there was a direct relationship between this aim and the Gulf War. Perhaps I was there simply to protect some minor, weak nation against a horrible and powerful foe. So I was still part of the blue forces, and evil Saddam Hussein, who was intent on having his way no matter what, was orange.

In my early twenties at RAF Biggin Hill, Kent,

where I was selected as an RAF officer, I was once asked during an interview if I would be prepared to go and drop the atom bomb and, if so, why would I do it. Without hesitation I answered yes. My reply was based on pure professionalism. If I was ordered to go, any doubt as to the validity of that order would question not only my own professionalism but also that of my senior officers and the politicians who had issued these portentous instructions to them.

I had been called on as a military man to do what was right and what the elected representatives of my country had decided must be done. If I had questioned their decisions, it would have been as insulting to those individuals as if someone had dared to question my own professional capability to go and deliver that horrible weapon of war against our enemies.

But as I got older I began to ask many more questions of myself. Certainly in the last few years, as I have realized that my flying career is coming to an end, I have begun to see the monetary value of my vastly expensive Tornado jet in a new perspective. It would perhaps cost about the same – around £20 million – to set up a small cottage hospital, and the running costs of my fighting machine would probably just about keep that hospital running.

If the threat to freedom and to Western Europe had lessened, so that each RAF squadron based in Germany could now do without just one Tornado, then, at no extra cost to the state, we could provide eight small hospitals back home in the UK.

I am not sure if I have become more of a pacifist,

but I can now see a very real peace dividend as the threat from the Russian bear decreases. There is no longer any doubt at all that our armed forces should reduce their presence in Europe, since the threat to the way of life that most of us hold dear has now diminished.

One of the main aspects of Bahrain, which I had not appreciated until I arrived there, was the complete difference between us and the local people. As a member of NATO and as a European, I could find many things of common interest to discuss with, say, a German or a Belgian: sport, a passion for cars, the weather or even family holidays – in short, a shared lifestyle that we all believe is worthy of preserving.

There is no doubt in my mind that in a European war, if I was fighting on German or Dutch soil, it would be for a real, tangible sense of freedom or liberty and it would be for a common cause. But I was totally unprepared for the fact that I had nothing at all in common with the Arabs.

Throughout my war I regularly spent time in conversation with Arabs, in bars and in restaurants, but I could never enjoy an argument with them. Whatever the subject, and whether it was before the war had begun or during it, everything was subject to the will of Allah. Almost anything you care to name would for them have an entirely different value from that placed on it by me or any of my comrades. And so I couldn't see how I could be there, based in Bahrain, fighting for the people in Kuwait and their ideals, since we had no common ideals.

Kuwait is a very small country, with no sense of democracy or even a political system that I could really understand or appreciate. The attitudes of the people, whether Kuwaitis or the labour imported from Third World Asian countries, were absolutely alien to us. We were fighting on behalf of an alien nation to achieve some very alien ideal. Despite all of this there was a very big undercurrent to my war. It was the Black Gold under the ground – oil had made this part of the world politically worth fighting for.

A year on, I can see that nothing has changed in the Middle East. The land itself is still almost entirely barren desert. Some parts of it are green and arable, but there was never enough to fight a war for. Certainly not enough to lay down my life for. But there was the Black Gold that all of the politicians so skilfully ignored as they roused the nations of the West to fight for the 'innocent' victims of tyranny.

What we were fighting for was the control of the world's oil supply – not for some high-principled humanitarian ideology at all. It was all about wealth and, what is more, it was about someone else's wealth. Perhaps I am too sceptical, but the only difference it would have made to my lifestyle would have been to put a few pence on the price of a gallon of petrol.

I still think that, even if the Iraqis had rumbled down into Saudi Arabia and taken over the oil resources there, perhaps ending up controlling half of the world's oil, possibly the situation would be the same as it is now.

Kuwait still has the same system of government,

the Saudis still have the same attitude to the West as they have always had and petrol is still going up in price at the same rate as it has always done.

And yet a few of my close friends and comrades simply no longer exist and my own attitudes to life have changed for ever. So I still ask myself what I was doing there.

During my very first bombing missions there were no politics of war for me. On every one of those early sorties we plotted our route to the target and our return. We were given our task and our requests for support from specialist American warfare equipment were invariably met.

Naturally, as the war progressed, the support that could be made available to us was often reduced and tasked to other missions and we were forced to cut our cloth accordingly. But later on, for some of the trickier missions, we continued to plan every second of the sortie according to the same high level of assistance from our allies. To guarantee our safe return we relied totally on that support.

On our fourth mission, an early-night sortie on 25 January, we would be heading out to bomb an oil-pumping station just north of Kuwait, inside Iraq. This mission was going to be very different from anything we had flown before. It was to be our very first excursion into 'Flak Alley' and we had decided to take the risk of flying straight into enemy territory rather than taking our usual sweep across Saudi Arabia.

For the first time during the conflict, we would

have to fly little more than 100 miles across the border, over enemy airspace, to reach our target. This was far less than the usual 300–400 miles over enemy territory just to reach our target without running the huge risk of being spotted and shot down over intense military activity.

We always used every tactic possible to confuse our enemy. By flying feint lines of advance or by flying forwards to a target in a zigzag formation, we could leave any enemy radar monitoring us only able to surmise what our outbound destination may be. Our hopes were that any waiting enemy armed with Triple A or SAM missiles would not be expecting us.

For this new profile I discussed at length with my team what the dangers would be. We would be spending less than half an hour in enemy airspace but flying over the heaviest defences outside Baghdad, which included thousands of Republican Guard troops. Provided we could get the very special American electronic warfare support that we needed, we decided it was worth going ahead with the mission as planned.

We would be flying along this heavily defended corridor of airspace in Iraqi territory and the great danger to our plan was that we would be running the grave risk of being picked up by enemy radar for the whole of that sortie. The very great advantage was that we would be spending a short time in Iraqi territory compared with the usual uncomfortable two hours.

We decided to go, for after all, there would

be more than enough American support to shield us from enemy eyes. Ours was another eight-ship formation and we were feeling confident about our battle skills. But within minutes of walking into our final brief we were told that the American support had been withdrawn and reallocated to another, much more valuable, bombing target. I was convinced that this would leave us hopelessly open to everything the Iraqis could throw at us. I began to contemplate the prospect of having breakfast next day with less than half the crew who had been lucky enough to survive what we were about to encounter.

I explained to our leaders after our brief that our entire plan had been based upon getting full support, and asked whether we could now have some vital extra time to replan our sortie over a longer, less dangerous route. My base commander listened in silence to my argument but then looked me hard in the face and said without hesitation, 'I'm ordering you to go.'

I could see the compassion in his eyes, for he was one of very few senior officers who openly expressed his emotions. But this time his deep concern for the eight aircrew who would shortly obey his order was overruled by the dictate that it was his duty to order me to go and it was mine to obey, whatever the consequences. His unspoken words were almost as important as the final orders he gave me. He did not say that every single aircrew who failed to return from the mission would be on his conscience for ever, but then he did not need to.

I had tried my damnedest to get that mission scrubbed and redrawn, since it simply did not deserve the risk. But there was nothing left for me to do except put on a brave face and speak to my boys about the new dangers that would now be out there to meet us. Of course, these would be far greater than if we had been given all the American air support we were hoping for, which would, with its squeaky electronics, completely 'whitewash' any enemy radars. But now, if those Iraqi radars were up and running, as they surely would be, they would see us all the way in and all the way out again. Most frightening of all, though, was knowing that they would also be able to draw on countless missile systems to engage us.

So, as coolly and calmly as I could, I ordered my boys to prepare for our next mission as planned. I knew there was no chance at all of our receiving the total support from our allies at the last minute, but still I had to offer that hope to my team as a few final words of encouragement. I suggested that there was still a slim chance that our support would turn up at the last minute, even though I knew there was no likelihood at all.

By the time we got to the Iraqi border we had been chatting to each other over the secure radio for some time. Apart from our own voices, the airwaves were almost silent; it was clear that there was very little else out there supporting our mission.

Amazingly, the mission proved to be the nearest thing to a complete doddle. Either the Iraqis were asleep or on holiday, or perhaps they had just had enough for one day. That is, until we got to our target and began dropping our bombs. As we dropped them off into the inky-black night something the size of a caravan came up alongside my cockpit and then gracefully made its meandering way back to earth, burning like some mobile furnace. I was delighted – I had hit my target all right!

But seconds later it seemed as though an Iraqi general's alarm clock had gone off, and all hell broke out. Everyone and his mate was firing at us and the sky lit up as though daybreak had been brought forward by half an hour. We all saw several missiles go off but at our altitude of 20,000ft they were failing to reach us. I knew that confidence was building up among the boys as I heard cries of 'You missed!' and 'You couldn't hit a barn door!'

But then a missile arced over my jet and exploded above us. That brought us all to our senses, and we realized that we weren't exactly flying above the flak but running home through a layer between it.

The most comforting call we could have hoped for came from the limited AWACS support team who had monitored our mission. The picture was clean; there were no enemy aircraft on our tail. As we radioed in to our base, Gary called that our mission had been successful, pausing, before adding 'extremely'.

Flak Alley was just a few hundred miles along the Tigris and Euphrates delta and in those first missions along there it was always guaranteed to light up like 4 July celebrations, because the enemy defences there were massive.

The run in to the target took just ten minutes flying at 600mph, and the run out again was just as fast as the jets would go. This nasty little strip of Iraq was also known as the 'Corridor of Fear'.

The oil depot targets were just a few miles south of Shaibah, Iraq's main airfield operation on the Kuwait–Iraq border. Every time we went back there we knew how much better we were getting at our job. You could see how the place was becoming well and truly trashed. After that first mission, which I had been convinced would be doomed, the place burned for four days and ended up just a landmark. We had done our job magnificently and towards the end of the war Flak Alley was quickly renamed Dead Man's Alley – there was nothing left there to hit.

We had got in that first time, smashed our target to smithereens and got out again unscathed and without too many real frights. But that mission was destined to be our first taste of the real military politics of war. We had trustingly based a plan on receiving support from another unit and when that support was not forthcoming we were still ordered to go.

I believe that experience taught me a lesson I would never forget for the rest of the war. I never again made a plan which relied so heavily on an input from an outside agency. If we could not do the work ourselves, then we would revise the plan and whatever support we then got for the sortie would become a bonus and would enhance an otherwise sensibly planned bombing mission.

It is true that I never wanted or even honestly expected to go to war, and I don't believe that any of us ever really did. But when it was our turn to go and fight we all did just that. We all had the dedication to go, not just because it was our job, but because it was also our chosen duty to carry out the business of war.

At some point during the conflict, as I began to consider the glaring differences between us and the people we were fighting for, I also started to appreciate that there is really little difference between a dedicated professional like myself and a highly paid mercenary who is prepared to fight for the highest bidder. My thoughts took me back to one of several chance meetings I once had with bomber pilots who had quit the RAF to become mercenaries.

I can still recall quite clearly how one day when I was standing at the bar of a pub in London I noticed a shady-looking character in the corner sipping a pint of beer. I had a copy of *Flight International* sticking out of my jacket pocket, which this chap must have spotted, because he came up and asked me if he could take a look at it. As he scanned the situations vacant column at the back of the magazine it became clear to me that he was a fellow aviator between jobs.

We chatted and he revealed to me that he had spent the previous two years flying an ageing stringbag of some sort, gun-running for a wealthy Middle Eastern client he had never actually met. I found his values amusing, for he was quite insistent that he would never have anything to do with drugs but he regarded arms dealing as perfectly OK, no matter whose war you happened to be fuelling.

He was like so many of these guys I had bumped

into along the way. They had flown fighter jets in various tinpot African or South American countries and it was obvious that they had enjoyed themselves, despite having no future prospect of a pension when they became too old for the job. I didn't respect them then, for after all they were bastardizing what I firmly believed to be a very honourable profession. But during the Gulf War I often began to see how I was no better and could even be regarded as the same as many of them.

True, my employer was still Her Majesty's Government and not some faceless pulp-fiction character at the other end of a phone. But, however hard I tried to be idealistic about my war and about what I was doing, it always boiled down to the fact that whoever was controlling the world's flow of oil was also controlling me. He was my paymaster.

My gradual and deepening dismay at my role in this war was only made worse by witnessing some of the men I had admired and respected for years suddenly transformed from kind, gentle, family men into dedicated killing machines.

During the very earliest days of the conflict, and as the war progressed, like many other men on the squadron I was deeply preoccupied with my own possible fate and with the direction in which my own life was going. But as time went on, my ability to cope with the new and deadly demands of war improved. I had more time to look around me and see how many of the others were coping with our circumstances.

As soon as the conflict began very few of the guys

found they could talk about their families and loved ones back home. Yet some of the boys were still regularly writing very long and loving letters home. But anything outside what was really happening at that precise moment in our lives suddenly became very private. People rarely talked about family matters and the conversation became very neutral if we were not discussing the business of war.

There was also a natural reluctance to dwell on the future or, for that matter, the past. Up until the outbreak of war I had easily found more than enough time to put in a few hours of studying for my civilian licence. I also regularly read at night: an autobiography, a history book or some other factual account of world events. All around our hotel quarters people were renewing some private interest in, say, steam engines or vintage aircraft.

But as soon as war broke out all those personal hobbies and interests were suddenly contained along with private family thoughts. It seemed that no one dared to let any new emotions escape. It was like Pandora's Box: once released, who knows what they could have done; they were safer kept locked away.

Just like me, many of my comrades changed their views and values in so many ways. Others had changed so much that I became frightened by what I saw. One young man in his mid-twenties, with whom I had flown many times, I had always regarded as a loving family chap who would have been truly shocked and outraged if he ever encountered brutal lack of compassion among his fellow men. He had a young son and his wife was expecting their second baby. I knew that his family always came first in his life and he had often made me feel guilty because I had always been an RAF officer first and foremost.

I believed we all shared that million-to-one hope that our bombs would never actually kill anyone, at least not innocent civilians. But that misconception was shattered by some of the pictures of our bombing missions seen on worldwide television and by video footage we later watched of what we had earlier witnessed in real life.

I have never been able to share the exultation of men like my young comrade, who quite clearly began to take enormous joy from seeing the devastating human effects of our work. For him it was almost the icing on the cake.

On 11 February we were tasked to carry out our fifth laser-guided bombing mission, known as pave-spiking, on a bridge in eastern Kuwait. It was along the main highway supply route from Iraq to Kuwait.

Spirits were running high for this sortie, for we had a cracking team of Buccaneers who were to guide our bombs on to the target. They were in the first division of Buccaneer crews, the target was a good ten miles from the nearest large town of Al Amarah and we had had several weeks of success without any further crew losses.

We planned a politically sensitive route as close to the Iranian border as possible without actually overflying it, although, at some points on our route, there was not much distance between the wing-tip closest to the border and an imaginary vertical line drawn from the border itself. We felt secure in the knowledge that neither Iran nor Iraq was likely to fire upon us, for fear of renewing recent hostilities between each other. The border itself provided us with an imaginary source of comfort.

Before our run in to the target, the twenty minutes we had spent flying along the border had been strangely quiet. Then we picked up the tone of another pilot's personal locator beacon. (We all carried one to alert Allied rescue forces to our position if we were shot down.) It may have been a signal from a recently downed aircraft but it was far more likely that Saddam Hussein's men were playing silly buggers with our kit to lure rescue crews into a trap. At the time, though, it was none of our business and we carried on after reporting the transmission to our airborne controller.

One of the aspects of this mission we had failed to even consider was that we would be hitting our target at precisely 8.22 a.m. and this would be around the start of a normal day's rush hour for any civilians with any business left to run.

I led the attack on the target with Bob Brownlow and his navigator Jack Calder in close formation. We released our bombs in a shallow dive from about 18,000ft. All six bombs were gone within microseconds and a little over thirty seconds later all six hit the target. The bridge was obliterated by thick black smoke, flames and debris spewing out in every direction.

In that instant before three tons of high explosive hit the bridge, I can vividly recall seeing vehicles and pedestrians making their way across it. They seemed to be strangely unaware of what was about to hit them. They stood no chance at all. For me, it was like playing God again with others' lives. I was all-powerful and at that precise moment their lives were in my hands and they were about to end.

From that point on I knew for sure I had killed people. I had watched it happen. In fact I hadn't just killed them; I had probably vaporized them. To my horror, when we returned to base to our debrief I watched the video footage of our mission.

I sat in complete silence as I watched the second bomb of my stick of three actually smash straight through the windscreen of a light-coloured saloon car as it was being driven across the bridge. Not only did I witness the terrible results of my work, but the world watched it with me on CNN television. At the time, of course, this was yet another job very well done and on the way home I didn't have time to think about what I had just seen from over the target.

The second wave of bombers had followed us one minute behind. Such was the carnage that we had created that they stood no chance of successfully releasing their bombs – they couldn't see the target, let alone hit it. I accept that this was war and if I killed someone I am sorry. I did not mean it personally, but war is war. It would have been fine if we could have simply taken out inanimate targets printed on a herringbone map, but that was not possible.

I'm not talking about the technical success of our mission but about the tragic and seemingly inevitable human losses that would have meant nothing to our aim of emasculating Saddam's military machine.

What I found very hard to accept was seeing other men who must have also watched all those people die, appear overjoyed by their deeds. I could not share the exhilaration of my young comrade, who was such a devoted family man. But others present at that debrief instantly recognized, as I had done, the tragedy of our actions. We were taking lives and they were probably very innocent lives.

I had assumed that everyone would feel the same way, that there was a kind of sickening aftertaste that came after all the backslapping that followed a triumphant sortie. But as we sat in that debrief and watched my second bomb crash straight through the saloon car's window, a hearty cheer went up. I looked around and was shocked to see that it came from men in my own team. If they are still happy now with the reaction they showed then, they are entirely different people from me and from the men I once thought they were.

If they have not already done so, they may nevertheless one day come to question the chilling form of pleasure that so clearly gave them a sense of purpose.

While I think we all displayed different reactions to the same events, I now firmly believe that the taking of life and the feeling of power at being able to do so almost fuelled a hitherto small fire that had been burning in the souls of some of my comrades for a very long time. Now, these men I had once believed I knew and trusted so well, were in a very new position. They had taken lives, they had a licence to kill, and I genuinely feared that this would become a raging inferno.

At the end of the war at least two guys I knew well had been taken over by some crazed desire to take life and not to stop. Suddenly, when they were finally told it was all over, their first reaction was not one of instant relief that they were now safe and could go home to their loved ones, that they would no longer be asked again and again to risk their lives. They were utterly frustrated and disappointed that their licence to kill had been revoked.

As a formation leader, it was my job to ensure the greatest possible safety of my team. I didn't ever truly feel invulnerable when I was out there flying bombing missions. But when people talked about aircrew losses, it never occurred to me that I was going to become one of those statistics. I would always feel sorry and saddened that the chances were, we would lose more crew. But I always believed those losses would be someone else's, not mine.

If any senior officer above me made a questionable decision I made it my business to request a change in our tactics or in our weapons load. I am sorry to say that the middle management of the RAF, the operations staff or senior officers at our Muharraq base, did not share any sense of responsibility to those who fought this war.

They never acted as decision makers or gave any of us any confidence in the orders they passed on from on high. These people were simply messenger boys who passed on detailed instructions from even higher authority. I don't recall one single decision being made by our operations executives. If ever I asked for a small change to the task or even a large alteration to the next bombing mission, they never once asked for my reasons, but simply passed on the request further up the chain of command.

This, of course, meant that no one would ever be able to appreciate the suggestions we made for a change in tactics. I was never face to face with an individual who might have been prepared to sanction my proposals or even explain directly to me why I had needlessly lost two crew members on a futile bombing mission.

I still cannot begin to understand why operations staff, often more senior and more highly paid than myself, became nothing more than glorified telephone operators. They would never make a decision on the strength of the first-hand information they had just received. Many of them could have easily been replaced by ordinary corporal telephone operators because that is all these officers really were. Needless to say, there have been one or two MBEs handed down for the good work these men did.

As for myself and my boys, I can vouch that we lived for the moment – it was all the time that we could afford. When we were relaxing we enjoyed a pretty wild time, and we put the same effort and energy into our work. For some of the time we experienced terrible fear, convinced that we were surely about to die. But on many other occasions there was total jubilation over a job that had been very well done.

It was not at all unusual to see one of the boys pull off a victory roll, just like those other brave flyers would perform in their Spitfires during the Second World War. We would often witness the odd spectacular landing as a crew would come into land and scorch up the runway to cheers and applause from the waiting ground crew. We all found our own way of putting the exuberance of our many achievements into some physical demonstration.

There were others who didn't live for the moment, for those seconds when we could have so easily slipped from life. They were the ones who were looking out for their careers, for their future after the war was over. You could imagine them already wearing their ribbons. Many of the senior commanders who went into battle with us were not working so much for their team as for that DSO ribbon they could pin on at the end of the war. It will have guaranteed them a place two ranks further up the hierarchy.

It amuses me even now that the more senior you become in the RAF, the braver you are. But, believe me, there were also very many brave young men whose contribution to the war has been almost completely ignored.

One young man, still in his twenties and based at Tabuk, flew more missions than anyone else in the Tornado force and I believe he also flew more operational missions than any of the RAF attacking forces. He was always there, this very pleasant young lad with an equally young wife waiting at home. He is a Flight Lieutenant and an exceptional pilot who notched up a staggering twenty-nine bombing missions, but he received no individual recognition whatsoever. He will get the same campaign medal as the cook who served him his bacon and eggs for breakfast before he went out on every one of those sorties. It is a great tragedy.

I had always imagined what it might be like if we ever went to war and what I expected that war to be like. I had always imagined that in a European theatre of war there would be far more national involvement than I ever saw in the Gulf. While I was fighting this war there would be difficulties in finding a shop open or food shortages that our own families would be expected to endure, just as countless families did during the First and Second World Wars.

Similarly, in the Gulf War, I had initially imagined that everyone would be involved in some way. There would be refugees clogging up the roads as they escaped from some advancing or retreating troops. They might be victims of bombing raids that had devastated their villages and homes. Or they would have relatives who were taking part in the war effort, fighting alongside the Allied armies.

But as the war went on, Bahrain maintained much of its hustle and bustle. The shops never closed and the restaurants stayed open. I felt almost as though I was a visiting member of a star football team. We would do our bit, and then have a few hours' relaxation before the next bombing mission.

It was easy to find some form of relaxation in Bahrain, for nothing closed, and it was as though the war was something that was happening in our minds.

It was hard for us to rationalize what we were doing. We would return from having been frightened or exhilarated, we could be happy or sad, but still nothing in Bahrain had changed.

Within weeks of the conflict starting, the anti-bomb-blast sticky tape that had been put over the windows was peeling off at the edges, and no attempt was made to replace it. The shops stayed open to take our money and the taxi drivers, who would never stop telling us how grateful they were to us, would still double the price of a fare because they believed we were all wealthy Westerners.

We were doing the fighting for the Bahrainis, for the Kuwaitis and for the Saudi Arabians. They had called in the professionals and we were going to do the job for them, and then be off. While I was always eternally grateful for the comfort that Bahrain offered us, our presence also raised the question of what we were doing there.

There were so many political issues at stake during this war that at times I hardly dared to wonder if our safety on many missions was ever considered at all. I accept that it was our job to risk our lives, and our duty to carry out bombing missions in the hope that we ultimately achieved victory. But there were times when other considerations were placed above our safety. That was surely wrong.

On 20 January – just three days after we had suffered the tragic loss of the two Johns – we were tasked to bomb a heavily defended airfield. Iraqi airfields were among the most hated of all our targets because we knew they were almost certainly backed up by an astonishing array of defences. There would be Triple A and SAM missiles to aim at us as we ran into and out of the target.

But to the north-west of this airfield there was a mosque, and if we had accidentally hit this it would have no doubt created enormous anti-Allied publicity for the enemy. At the planning stage we were reminded countless times that if there was any risk of us damaging the mosque, then we were not to deliver our ordinance. This Muslim place of worship must survive our attack without so much as a cracked slate. We were ordered to carry out a mission with an almost impossible constraint.

We had just met our new wingmen, who were to replace our lost boys. They had arrived in the Gulf just nineteen hours before they flew to war with us.

This second sortie was to be flown under the comforting shroud of darkness. We would be taking off as the sun set and overflying the target in total darkness. There was very little moon that night, which came as a huge relief to us all. We were nervous both about the sensitivity of this task and because we would be an eight-ship formation flying for the first time in a medium-level attack on the airfield. We had all only ever flown out to war in the safety of low-level flying, which hid us from enemy radars. Nor did we have anywhere near as much Allied support as we had had on 17 January.

Then, as we prepared for take-off, we learned that our two Johns were alive. They had been captured but they were safe. I knew in my heart I would be sharing a beer with the two of them when all this was finally over. I went off again into the night with a huge sense of relief. We would see them again if we came out of this one alive.

My four jets would lead this mission, with another formation, led by Greig Thompson and Bob Sinclair, both from RAF Marham in Norfolk, at the rear.

The first jet I climbed into suddenly developed a technical fault and Gary and I just had time to clamber into one of the waiting spares on the pan. She was Debbie and she became my favourite. From then on I would do everything I could to fly every sortie in her.

We launched, as planned chasing the sunset over Saudi Arabia before turning north to make our attack. By the time we crossed into Iraq we had the protective veil of night around us. There was also the comfort of the voice of an airborne controller telling us the picture was clean – there were no enemy aircraft on his radar screens. We were also buoyed up by the sounds from our radios of American fighters positioning to shepherd us through to our target. They were ready to do their damnedest to chase away any would-be aggressor.

This medium-level sortie was new to us and our Tornadoes. This was not their natural environment and it was something we had only spent a little time practising during training. Refuelling proved challenging too. We were flying at night with our lights switched off to avoid detection. There was now no more than the glow from another jet's exhaust to guide each other. Our Tornadoes were as heavy as we had ever flown them as we headed north, deep into enemy airspace.

The night was strangely quiet as Gary and I concentrated on our own sectors of the sky, looking for any last-minute threats. We continued on northwards and Gary gave me a final reminder that this had to be an accurate attack. If we deviated to the left by just 4km we would hit the mosque.

As we continued in to the target, our main radar failed and we would no longer be capable of identifying the target to aim our weapons. Seconds later our number three reported the same problem and as we moved in the entire formation performed an aerial ballet. I changed places with our number four and number three swapped with number two.

We were operating in total darkness except for the distant glow from an aircraft engine to help slot each jet into its new position. In order to be guided by that friendly glow, we had to be directly behind each jet. A mixture of luck and judgement helped us into place. The adrenalin was racing as I nudged Debbie in behind Mark Paisey in number four.

As we ran in on the last minute, I called Mark on our closed radio to give me a precise signal when he was about to drop his bombs.

I was now blind; we could see nothing other than with our own eyes in that blanket of darkness. Mark was to give me a countdown of three-two-one as he released his bombs on the target. That would be my signal to let my bombs go, hopefully bang on target too.

As we ran in I realized we had no better technology

91

than any Second World War bomber. Gary was equipped with a map and a stopwatch. He didn't even have the guiding light of the moon to help him direct us on to the target. No more than ten seconds to target I heard his reassuring voice from the back, 'OK Pablo, we're running in.'

We looked out to see that all below us was quiet. The target area itself was swathed in mist. Then there was a whoop and a scream, followed by the sight of a dull glow as Mark Paisey and Mike Toft's engines vanished off to the right.

They had obviously just dropped their bombs and run for it. We had microseconds to go and I found time to laugh at how our carefully worked out timing had just fallen apart.

Mike Toft had been working to his limits to offload those bombs on the target, but then he must have thought: Crikey, I've got to tell Pablo to go in. His desperate screams were enough to make me laugh out loud as I pressed the button and delivered four tons of high explosive.

I put my aircraft on its ear and just prayed there was enough room for us to run out behind number four.

Gary called out, 'Impact any time now, Pablo.' Then as I dropped the right wing and turned ninety degrees for home, the blanket of fog below us transformed into flashes of brilliant orange and red.

The scene below was just like something from a Second World War movie. We could hear the crump, crump, crump as our bombs smashed into the target. It was like dropping paint into a bucket of water which instantly diffused into an expanding circle filled with red and yellow glows.

As the other boys ran in their bombs joined mine, some finding even juicier targets. There was a pinprick, a sharp, brilliant-white glow and then a large, expanding circle of yellow followed by another of orange. Then, in the middle of all this, there was a ripple of red running off in a flash of fire heading skywards and then bursting off through the misty layer that was trying to conceal the massive explosions below.

Fuel and oil dumps exploded in a staccato series of pinpricks. Then there was another burst of pinpricks as the enemy awoke and began firing off their Triple A almost at random. Within seconds the sky was a mass of Triple As snaking up towards us. Strangely, I didn't feel frightened. I was just in awe of this massive fireworks display. But then it seemed that we were flying into an immense, burning cauldron. Gary screamed out on our intercom, 'Make like a shepherd. Let's get the flock out of here!'

On our right I saw a missile plume snaking up and on the left there was another. We were like spectators watching a very dangerous tennis rally. As the missiles crossed in a perfect arc in front of us, Gary called to me, 'Christ, did you see that?' 'No. And I didn't see that either!' I replied.

As we all raced back to our refuelling tankers I looked back to see the second wave of our delayed bombs still exploding. As we raced south it was clear we had done our job well. We flew for nearly five minutes while still seeing the satisfying glow of explosions going off well after our bombs hit the target.

We had managed to get eight aircraft safely out of the target and now Gary was using his map and stopwatch to get us safely out into Saudi airspace. His reckoning was bang on as usual, and within seconds we could switch on our lights to search for the refuelling tankers. There they were, in a race-track orbit, waiting for their chicks to come home to roost. As I was about to disconnect my refuelling probe I looked around and saw a fourth aircraft hooked on to the same tanker. In the confusion, five jets had hooked up to one tanker. In peacetime this would have been a catastrophe worthy of months of investigation, but we couldn't have cared less. In our euphoria we were just happy to all be going home together.

As we turned away for home we could see the smiling faces of the tanker crews by the glow of their controls. They gave us a cheery wave home.

Later that night American B52 bombers went in and reported the airfield was in ruins and that nothing would be flying out of there again. We were just relieved that no one reported any other bomb damage in the area. We had just risked our lives and yet we were more relieved that we had carried out our task without so much as knocking one slate off that bloody mosque.

Ironically, before the war was over, we discovered that Saddam's own troops had gone in to trash the place, razing it to the ground. So much for the politics of war.

We were delighted by our incredible success. It was such a wonderful contrast to the dejection we had all felt after our first mission only three days before. As we stood around on the pan congratulating each other, Mike Toft came out with the immortal line: 'Dad, you were fantastic. How was I?'

I looked around to see the wisps of smoke from the jet exhaust and the dull glow from hot engines. There were little wires hanging down where there had once been bombs. We had just delivered 64,000lb of high explosive and every bomb a hit!

This sortie was one of many examples of the political implications of our task being given astonishing priority over the mission's success.

We often found it difficult to recognize our own individual value as a human being and as a warrior. At the end of each sortie the TV cameras would be there with reporters hanging on to our every word. They would drink in the success or the partial failure of each mission. We all knew that whatever we said would almost certainly make world headlines.

We would be quoted on television, then played and played again on video recorders, reaching millions of homes around the world. We were of global importance and much of the free world was listening to our every word.

Yet within a matter of hours a new briefing would be going on where senior officers made us realize our views and suggestions for a mission were almost certainly going to be disregarded. Seniority and rank took precedence every time. We may have been worth listening to a few hours before but now we had no value. We were so many tools, used to carry out a job.

My formation was taken out of front-line flying missions from 30 January to 1 February, to help perfect laser-guided bombing techniques from medium altitude. This was an adaptation of techniques which involved the use of ancient Buccaneer jets, with their outmoded radar systems, to guide our bombs on to the target.

In Germany, a few of us had occasionally been given the chance to train with the Buccaneers, but only ever from low-level attack profiles. In a couple of days we had to perfect a system of attack from medium level. This had been calculated to work – on paper at least!

Of course, the new tactics were also intended to accurately deliver our bombs on to targets where our dumb, conventionally guided bombs would run the risk of killing and maiming countless people. We were given a clean slate and just a few ideas. The learning curve was almost vertical as we flew endless simulated attacks on our own airfield, ready for the real thing.

The first of these 'pave-spiking' missions we were to fly, on 2 February, just had to be a success. We had practised this profile countless times and we had got to know the voices of our Buccaneer mates. When we eventually flew the mission against an Iraqi bridge, the weather forecast was excellent for the target area, we had reserve Tornadoes and

Buccaneers to hand and we knew every inch of the route.

I led a six-jet sortie alongside a team of Buccaneers. We were equipped with pictures of our target from every conceivable angle, which would be precision bombed within thirty seconds of running in.

We flew in broad daylight and then into dense cloud, which meant we had to fly in incredibly tight formation, with no more than a wingspan between three jets in each formation. We needed to fly so close because the two Buccaneers who made up the formation had such ancient navigation systems that they needed to physically see us. Tornadoes could split up and then meet up again because we had confidence in our precision navigation kit, even in dense cloud. But if a Buccaneer lost sight of us, the next time we would see him, with luck, would probably be in the bar.

It was physically and mentally draining to fly so dangerously close. Running in to the target, I knew that just one enemy missile could have taken out three of us at once. We had no room to manoeuvre.

With about four minutes and fifty miles to go to our target, the skies just opened up. We had left the sanctuary of the cloud behind us and with only a minute off target the Triple A and tracer was flying off around us. The concentration of fire was incredible and there was no room to be scared about what was happening on the ground. We just eased into the target, giving our Buccaneer the precise bomb range so that he could guide his laser TV camera on to the site.

If the pilot was happy I would release my bombs, but we always knew there was a chance he would pick up enemy fire or aircraft. That was time for him to scream: 'Stop, stop, stop', so that we could pull up and get out of the target area as fast as we could.

The mission was a huge success. It was pure weapons aiming to perfection and led to dozens more laser-guided missions. We had blasted our target and now had a couple of seconds spare to concentrate on our own preservation.

The Buccaneers had done the fine tuning and our bombs did the work. When we heard the Buck crews call 'Splash' we knew we had done the job to perfection.

It seemed strange as we flew back that the cloud that had been our enemy while we were flying in such tight formation was now our friend. Running back home from the target, we were now 'singletons' again and very vulnerable until we reached that cloud cover.

The videotape showing us decimating the bridge was flashed around the world. We had been given the best support, the best aircraft in reserve and the most able Buccaneer crews. They were the cream of their profession and did their job brilliantly.

But within days of that first laser-guided mission life became more and more difficult. We were tasked to bomb tougher targets and yet it was the luck of the draw if we managed to secure an experienced Buccaneer crew for the mission. Everyone worked to the best of their ability but there is no doubt that many of those crews were out of their depths during the war.

They were being tasked in with us when they had little more than two years' experience on the squadron. But we had shown the public how good we were, so it no longer mattered. We had now been placed a little further down the priority ladder.

Word came down that all Buccaneer crews must fly the same number of missions, regardless of their ability. But the fact was that some of these guys were superb at their job and should have been tasked to fly as many missions as their metabolism allowed.

I had flown in the same four-ship formation for months until we lost the two Johns. Now we had to look at the programming roster to see who would be joining us on pave-spiking missions. They were often guys we didn't know and had never seen before. The roster soon became more important than guaranteeing our success at getting through to the target and getting ourselves home again. It was hard to appreciate what the priorities were after all.

I never honestly felt worthy of the tremendous world attention or the accolades that came from a proud public back home. But there were also times when we believed that the military system we belonged to had little regard for us. Many aspects of this conflict brought home to us the folly of other wars, such as the World Wars and the Falklands War. But I often reflect that we never truly learn from our many repeated mistakes.

My own attitudes have changed enormously since I first flew out to war. In many ways I believe I let my own family down by going to war. I stopped writing to Sheila and the kids after the day that war broke out. Yet she still has the letters that I wrote up to that day. They were some of the most feeling and deeply personal letters I have ever written in my life. When I was on detachments she could expect to receive only one or two notes if I was away for a month or two. But one day in early January, out in the Gulf, I wrote to her four times and each one was a very long letter.

I think I honestly felt I had let my family down by going to fight. But I'd always been a loyal, patriotic person. I stand for the National Anthem and, to me, Her Majesty the Queen is a very real embodiment of our English heritage. This is something that is admired by very many other nations and I believe it is well worthy of their respect and appreciation. Loyalty to my Queen and country is very easily translated into loyalty to my wife and children and to my values.

Yet here I was risking my own life and the lives of many of my fellow men who had placed great trust in me and my navigator, Gary Stapleton. But I was not defending my Queen or my country, nor my wife or children. They were not at any risk other than that of losing a husband and father who loved them dearly. I think I let them down because I never found the courage to say that I would not go. I could not find the strength to say, 'No, this is not my war, it's not my fight. This is someone else's war. Give it to them to fight.'

During our briefings I had always impressed upon my men that if the risks were anything but acceptable, they must turn around and get out. Not because they had to consider what they were really fighting for, but what would be lost if they were lost. Naturally, I meant that they must always consider their feelings for their own families. If ever enough equipment on their jet became unserviceable to make it less than 100 per cent effective, they must turn around and come home.

Yet on several occasions Gary and I went to war with no radar and major pieces of kit totally unworkable. I still don't know why we did that when we were already taking enormous risks with our lives.

We regularly bombed heavily defended bridges or airfields and the Iraqis would have known these were important targets. But they just didn't know when we were going to hit them, and for most of the time that was the single biggest factor on our side.

And yet I still did things which I always vowed I would never do, and I still can't explain why. I know that on one occasion I could have been responsible for losing my life. I still cannot believe my stupidity.

On our ninth bombing mission, on 8 February, I flew into battle feeling very different. I couldn't quite put my finger on what was missing. We flew off at the crack of dawn with four jets and two Buccaneers to hit another bridge a few miles west of Baghdad. The disadvantages were that it was close to very heavy defences and it was a major enemy transportation route.

As we flew across the Saudi desert I suddenly became aware of why I felt so different that morning.

I didn't feel scared at all: for the first and only time I had not taken with me that mind-numbing sense of fear which I had become so used to. I didn't even consider what we might be facing as we refuelled and set off over the enemy border.

As we ran in there was very little flak and I began to feel strangely invulnerable. I felt that if the engines stopped I could just clamber out of the cockpit and walk. I had to force myself to think that I wasn't God or Superman, for if I couldn't accept that I knew I would surely die.

On our very next mission, on 9 February, I learned how to feel scared again as we went into a daylight dive attack on a fuel depot north of Kuwait. The target was almost completely obscured by cloud and we had been briefed not to attempt a target we were not certain we could hit, to avoid killing innocent people.

As we went in I could see our bombs were smashing up the target and we all cheered as Steve Barnes scored a direct hit on a fuel container, sending up a massive ball of flame. In that instant I thought: I can do that. Just watch me, lads.

I rolled my aircraft in for another dive on the target but it all seemed to be happening too quickly and I was no longer in control. In a split second I suddenly realized I could have left it too late for me and Gary.

I burst out through the clouds and I had the target in my sights as I released my bombs. I climbed as fast as I could as the enemy opened up on us with a massive burst of fire. I hadn't just flown through cloud, there was also flak and Triple A and I had to make our escape through it all.

As I shot up through the cloud, pointing towards the blazing sun, I was grateful to be alive, sorry for being stupid and relieved and respectful that I had regained my sense of fear.

When we got back to our base I could sense that everyone's nerves were jangling. We'd managed a hell of a lot without any further Tornado losses and we had all begun to feel that time could be running out on us again.

That night I wanted to go home, I was fed up with the war. We had survived nine missions against all odds and we had lost two good men on the way. Our new laser-guided bombing tactics were working and the hits against us were getting less.

But after that ninth raid I knew I had gone too far. I hadn't been scared when I should have been terrified. That thought really frightened me.

# 4

# Dealing with Fear

Only once in my life before the first two months of 1991, had I ever experienced real, abject fear as a result of my profession as an RAF pilot. That was on 29 July 1983, when I was involved in a mid-air collision at the end of my tactical weapons training course at RAF Chivenor in Devon.

I had flown the sortie as a matter of luck and I have always believed that my survival was also a matter of luck. Nigel Risdale was booked to fly the sortie and he would have occupied the seat that I took – until moments before the final briefing, when he was assigned to another task. The flight was offered to me and I grabbed at the chance of a few extra hours up in the air, as I had not been programmed to fly that day.

It was a glorious Friday afternoon and I can still remember clearly that it was also a special day. This was to be the last day that flying suits would be allowed to be worn in the officers' mess bar. We had even arranged a drinks party for that evening to celebrate this final day of freedom. I had managed to scrounge as many flying suits as I could find and they were all hanging on a rail just outside the bar. This was all part and parcel of RAF tradition and there would be no excuse for anyone who came in not wearing one of our green flying suits, by order of the aircrew on the base.

After forty-five minutes of being airborne I could only think how blissful life really was. I was doing the job I had always wanted to do and it was one of the greatest pleasures of my life. Everything was going swimmingly up there until suddenly, in our windscreen, another aircraft, which looked the size of a jumbo jet, appeared. It was followed by a loud and sickening crunch and then a roar of air as a gaping hole was torn into the cockpit canopy, which was now also shattered. Pieces of the canopy were falling away and most of the instrumentation was gone.

I didn't even know if Pete Sheppard, who was sitting in the front seat of the aircraft, was alive or dead. As the noise from the debris breaking away began to die down, a reassuring voice from the front seat called out, 'Are you all right, Pablo?'

I was fine at that moment. Professionalism just took over as I grabbed for a scrap of paper which was tucked away in one of the pockets of my flying suit. I began to note down the engine instrument indications that were still working and checked through the panel of warning signals. Then I peered through the shattered canopy to the wing surfaces and twisted my head back as far as I could see to try to assess the state of the fuselage behind my cockpit. It may seem hard to believe but I was actually making those detailed notes for the benefit of other pilots who would fly this type of aircraft in the future.

Sure, I was scared. But I wasn't going to allow that fear to take a hold of my thoughts. I was still alive, and I was going to do my damnedest to climb out of there alive. We still had our radio and I had sent a Mayday call back to our base. We were both relieved to hear over the radio that the guys who had hit us, an Iraqi trainee pilot and his instructor, had safely ejected and were on their way to hospital for medical checks.

In front of me, Pete Sheppard seemed so calm and collected and when we later spoke he confessed that he was amazed how cool and together I had sounded. But inside I was experiencing for the first time the awful, gut-wrenching fear that was to be my constant companion in the early months of 1991.

Tracts of wire and hydraulic pipes which had once been so neatly packed away in the nose of the fuselage were now trailing wildly from the battered bulkhead.

Malcolm Howell, who was up flying another Hawk jet that afternoon, had come within about 100 yards of our stricken jet to take a look at the damage. We radioed to him to take a closer look at our aircraft in an attempt to assess the total damage, but he refused to come any nearer. I don't blame him: there were bits peeling off the fuselage all the time and anything could have fallen off and damaged his own jet. Pete's feet were actually sticking out in the airstream and Malcolm cautiously informed us that the front of the aircraft forward from the canopy was completely missing.

We'd lost about 4ft of aircraft, but Pete Sheppard still managed a joke. During the impact the under-carriage had lowered itself, the two main wheels were indicating green and the nose wheel was showing red. This indicated that the aircraft would not be safe to land. Pete casually pointed out that he would not be managing a 'green' landing that afternoon.

Much of what is left of that nose wheel is now a table lamp in my home. I discovered its remains in a field at Hamworthy in north Devon, about forty miles from where I finally ejected.

We were facing a major problem. Pete was anxious to eject to safety, but I had always known throughout my fast-jet career that the ejection seat is not designed to provide a comfy ride. It is designed to save lives but the possibility of receiving a back injury or some other lifelong damage is very real. I have known guys who have ejected to complete safety with hardly a scratch to testify to their experience. Others will spend the rest of their years confined to a wheelchair. I did not want that to happen to me. For the moment, anyway, I was safe and comfortable still flying around, albeit in half a jet.

If I had tried to land the jet there was a good chance that I would have got out unmarked, but for Pete there was a grave risk of injury from the aircraft either ploughing into the ground or flipping over. In either situation he would probably have been killed.

Finally, we decided that Pete should eject while I tried to land what was left of our jet. I took over the controls from the back seat, which was something

I had done many times before. But this time the aircraft felt strangely light and far more sensitive than I had ever been used to. I began to consider all the possibilities of attempting to land back at Chivenor. How would the aircraft react now it was so light in front?

We were about fifteen miles off the extended centre line of Chivenor's runway when it was time for Pete to eject. It was now twenty minutes since the collision yet it seemed like hours. A few moments later George Lee, the Wing Commander Operations at Chivenor, called me on the radio to ask if there was anything I wanted to say. Of course, I knew immediately that he meant did I have any last messages for those left on the ground if everything went wrong for me.

I knew that Sheila would be with the children; Michael was just three and Ellie was still in nappies. But they would probably all be together having a lovely time on the beach. There was something I wanted to say, for them, but something held me back. I didn't want the world to be privy to some last word to my family, a private thought that was only meant for my wife and children.

I said nothing and in the next few seconds Pete ejected and then the engine cut out. I tried desperately to relight it but by now the aircraft had transformed into a mechanical bucking bronco. There was no choice now but for me to eject. I grabbed the handle and pulled hard.

There were two loud bangs and I momentarily lost consciousness. Then there was nothing but peace and quiet after the roaring sounds that had poured in through the shattered cockpit. Here I was, suspended under a gorgeous silk canopy about 8000ft from the ground. Pete later told me that as he came down in his parachute about half a mile from me he could hear me singing and laughing uncontrollably. I landed totally unscathed and was flying Hawks again four days later.

But I had tasted fear. There was fear from the moment of our collision to the moment when I chose to eject. That fear had been with me in the cockpit for some twenty minutes. It was to return as a constant companion during the Gulf War. It was there at varying levels of intensity but it never truly went away.

I was quite pleased with the way I had conducted myself that summer's afternoon in north Devon. There were plenty of congratulations and much backslapping from my colleagues. They didn't need to know just how scared I had been. I had saved my own skin, even though the piece of hardware I had wrestled to bring home was now resting on the bottom of Barnstaple Bay.

Years later that experience became a yardstick. I had been terrified in the air and I had still managed to pull through.

During the Gulf War my mind often flashed back to the autumn of 1974, when I was learning to fly in a jet Provost trainer. I had joined my course mates for a night out at a disco in York, near our station. We were the young, thrusting pilots of tomorrow and we were out to impress. I can recall chatting up one young teenage girl and offered to buy her a drink.

As we sat trying to talk above the din from the music I proudly told her that I was a fighter pilot. Of course I wasn't, not then, but I was determined to become one. She looked at me with round eyes full of amazement as she asked me in her broad Yorkshire accent, 'Oooh-er, a fighter pilot eh? Don't you get really scared?'

I laughed as I nonchalantly replied, 'No, I never get scared. You don't have time to get scared.'

Nearly fifteen years later that ridiculous and pompous statement came bubbling to the surface as I sat in a briefing at Muharraq. I had to withdraw those words wholeheartedly. I had lied. Of course I get scared and now I was scared all the time.

When it finally came to flying to war I had learned much more about myself and about the men who trusted me to take the lead. I was no longer 'Sir' or 'Squadron Leader Mason'. I was Pablo to all of them. I really didn't care what the guys called me as long as they followed me, but not in blind obedience like a bunch of sheep. I wanted them to come with me to war because they wanted to fight alongside me and for us to be together as a team.

I just happened to be the most experienced officer in the formation, so it was natural for me to be at the front. I hoped that they also saw me as the one they could trust to bring them home again, if that was at all possible.

I saw other styles of leadership around me: dynamic, aggressive leadership where everything would be done one way regardless of the ideas that may have been put up by juniors. I could see that they felt stifled and sat upon because this iron fist in an iron glove could not tolerate any dissension, which would only be seen as a weakness, some kind of crack in the team's ability to carry out the job.

Whatever team I was going to take to war, I wanted the best ideas to come from them, and for them to trust that each would be heard and considered. My rank was not on the line, but our lives were, and they were more valuable than anything.

XV Squadron was to provide twelve crews for the Gulf. That meant three teams of four aircrew and at normal manning levels we had around sixteen pilots and sixteen navigators from which to make our selection. We had our youngsters; young men who had not been in the RAF for more than two or three years and had come to the squadron straight from conversion training to fast jets. They were keen to go but they just did not have the calibre of some of the older hands who had flown for years. It followed that the twelve pilots and twelve navigators who were considered the most experienced or able almost chose themselves.

The next problem was allocating each name to a four-ship formation, a composition they would certainly fly as a team throughout the war. The task of crew selection fell to the squadron's most senior pilot, Gordon Buckley. He spent days painstakingly trying to put together strong teams. I never envied him his task, for he received constant hassle from many of us who were anxious to end up flying both with people we rated and actually liked. Each of us wanted the best possible chance of success and survival, so we all took a healthy interest in who would occupy the other seat in our two-man war machine.

The squadron commander finally decided that each formation should be led by the most experienced crews. This also meant that younger lads like John Peters and John Nichol would not be able to fall back on the experience of a more capable crewman in the other cockpit; they would have to fly together and trust in my leadership. I was not disappointed that they both joined my formation, even though they were the least experienced members of my team. They were lacking in experience but they were keen and enthusiastic, and I liked and admired them both.

If I was to rely on my own strong leadership for the preservation of all of us, I decided that I wanted a damn good navigator with me. At a very early stage I asked my seniors if I could fly with Gary Stapleton, the son of the famous fifties bandleader Cyril. I didn't know Gary very well and I'm not sure that many of us really did. He has a certain arrogance but in his pursuit of excellence as a first-class navigator he has never suffered fools gladly. He is aggressive, selfish and entirely self-confident, and I knew that I could trust him and rely on his judgement.

On 27 August 1990 I had just returned to RAF Laarbruch after a successful training exercise with Gary. He had come back to his usual mountain of paperwork when I wandered into his office and casually asked if he would be happy to go to war with me. He just looked up from his desk and said that he thought that would be rather fun and then carried on writing up a memo. It was to be the start of a very special relationship that continued throughout the conflict.

Gary and I have shared confidences and secrets that I know we will never share with anyone else, not even our loved ones. I realized that at any stage during the war there would also be problems for us. We are both strong personalities, and while we are of similar age and outlook on life, we are also very different men who value life differently. But in the months ahead we were to become totally reliant on our relationship with each other in the air.

I was glad to have the team I was given. Although I had tried hard not to give Gordon Buckley a tough time while he decided on the formation of crews, I gave him a verbal list of people with whom I definitely did not want to go to war. It was not because they were no good at their job or that they were weak characters. It was simply that I didn't like or respect them.

I was delighted to be taking on John Peters and John Nichol as my wingmen. They were new to the game, but brave and keen to learn.

My number three crew, Chris Lunt ('Lunty') and Colin Ayton ('Stroppy Jock') were in the same mould but with the priceless gift of years of experience.

Mike Toft was joined as my number four by Mike

113

Paisey ('Mr Pastry'), who had arrived as an unknown quantity from 20 Squadron.

After the two Johns were tragically shot down, our new wingmen, Bob Brownlow and Jack Calder, joined us from IX Squadron on 20 January. Within hours they became as much a part of the team as if they had spent all those months with us during the build-up to the war.

Between us all we built up a sixth sense which I know helped us through many tricky moments. It was almost unbelievable how we could all transmit a thought to each other and know that it had been fully understood without one word having been uttered. This astonishing rapport began to manifest itself towards the end of November, just before we flew out to the Gulf. I first noticed it as we were training in the air and trying to achieve the best possible formation positions.

I would chivvy John Peters to move up a little way or back a little on my wing as we came to a turning point on our route. Perhaps because of unexpected bad weather or because of the need to correct our timing, we had to alter our plans or simply change direction. On the radio, Gary would tell John when to make the turn, giving a new compass heading to take up. At times like this the radio chatter between all four crews would be almost incessant. But as the days wore on and the situations we flew became more complex, that chatter almost stopped.

At any time I could look across my wing at John and perhaps I would see him slightly out of position. As if he had just read my thoughts, he would move

DEALING WITH FEAR

up or back to correct his jet. He just knew when he
had to make a turning point to regain a timing line
or make better use of the terrain.

Very soon I could look over my shoulder and see
the rest of my team making the same precise moves
without one word of instruction over the radio.
In fact, I often found myself making meaningless
conversation just to let the boys know that I was
still there.

Sceptics may say that my team was just becoming
very accomplished at the job. But it was far more
than that: we were learning to live as a team together.
Every one of us possessed a natural desire to save his
own skin. But together we could perhaps protect and
save each other.

That sixth sense or extrasensory perception shared
by the eight men in my team quickly spread to our
lives on the ground. In the comfort of the officers'
mess, one of the lads might mention that he was
hungry, only to discover that his fellow crewman
had already gone off to find him a sandwich. And
I remember sitting at home in Germany wondering
if one of the lads might fancy a beer. Before I could
get out of my armchair the phone rang and it was
Mike Toft's cheery voice saying, 'Hi Pablo, fancy
a beer?'

By early December we had moved to the Sheraton
Hotel in Bahrain, where we shared rooms as crews.
We were like an extended family with me and Gary
at the head. I very soon became known as 'Dad' and
early on Gary, much to his horror, was nicknamed
'Mum', which the lads later changed to 'Uncle'.

115

Those who shared rooms became like long-married couples, squabbling about who was squeezing the toothpaste in the wrong place and over whose turn it was to make the beds.

Gary was and still is noted for his sartorial elegance. He would buy two pairs of identical trousers and insist they were different in some way. His wife, Sheena, made me promise not to allow him to use his credit cards while we were in Bahrain, but there was no way I could stop him, despite our arguments. He would spend as much on a new shirt as I would pay for a suit, yet here we were living together. If we were going out for the evening, he would always give me a once-over or a quick brush down to make sure that I was smart enough to be acceptable in his company.

In the last few weeks before war broke out, we did all we could to improve our chances of survival. There always seemed to be some aspect of our training, or even a visit to another part of the station, that would somehow help our preservation if the worst finally did happen.

During the first two weeks of January we were still running something of a training routine. It was never difficult to gain the attention of my boys, because anything I was trying to show them was almost certain to play some part in preserving their lives. I encouraged them to visit the various sections of the station at Muharraq, since they could perhaps glean a little more information about the task they were about to do. At the same time they could make themselves known to all the other people there who were part of that massive war effort. It may have been possible for them to share whatever they could of their emotions and their fears with either a ground crewman or one of the nurses at the war hospital.

We got to know quite a few of the nurses who were working at the base hospital. There was a professional reason for this: we all wanted to know what sort of treatment we could expect if we were shot and yet managed to get back home, albeit badly injured.

Just a ten-minute walk from our operations block at Muharraq airfield was the war hospital. I went there early one morning, just days before the conflict began, to find neat rows of beds stretching along makeshift hospital wards and saline drips already hooked up, waiting for the first casualties. The operating theatres were ready; they had been sterilized, sanitized and sealed shut, and would only be opened up when the first victims of war were rushed in.

I was a frequent visitor to the hospital, where I met up with some of the nurses for a cup of tea and a chat, but after we had flown our first few war missions I never went there again until it was all over.

I was shocked when I met some of the younger nursing staff, boys and girls of no more than seventeen or eighteen. They sat around nervously in little groups, clearly terrified at the prospect of facing legions of horribly injured men. They had no idea what to expect and so they feared the worst. Not one of them had ever seen a bullet wound and the prospect of caring for victims of bomb and chemical gas attacks had become a terrible nightmare to them.

But there were also dedicated and highly trained professionals to lead these wide-eyed youngsters. Many of the younger staff had still to receive formal medical training but they would be there to bring in the casualties and probably to take the remains out. Those young kids knew they would be the very first to deal with hundreds, if not thousands, of incoming casualties.

In the event, the hospital probably dealt with only four or five casualties during the whole war. But I just wonder how those youngsters coped with their fears and are overcoming them even now? Their war never actually happened, as it did for us. I flew to war and fought my battle. There are plenty of ghosts that still refuse to be buried for many of my comrades.

On 13 February Gary and I led one of the most demanding and frightening sorties of our entire war. It was certainly a case of being asked to bite off far more than we could chew. We were tasked to attack an airfield forty miles west of Baghdad. It was one of those horrible, heavily defended targets that had everyone who had gone before us coming back with horror stories. But not only had we been tasked to attack this airfield: we also had to go on to bomb yet another airfield, sixty miles west of Baghdad. If we got through that, we could come home.

Like many of the aircrew, I am a superstitious person. It was the thirteenth of the month and this was also to be Gary's and my thirteenth mission. Unfortunately, Debbie, the jet we had trusted so

My children, Eleanor and Michael.

Asleep aboard an RAF Hercules en route to the Gulf.

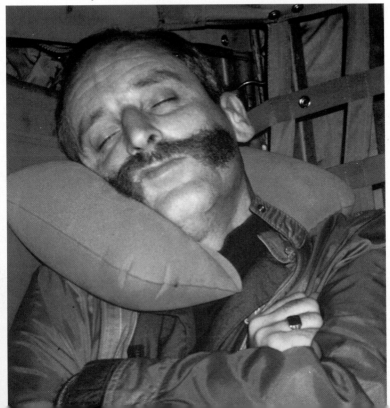

With Gary Stapleton, my navigator, in a Tornado cockpit.

My formation before hostilities began. Left to right: Chris Lunt (Lunty), Colin Ayton (Stroppy Jock), John Peters, Mark Paisey (Mr Pastry), Mike Toft (Tofty), Gary, me and John Nichol.

After the war. Left to right: Chris Lunt, Colin Ayton, Gary, me, Jack Calder, Mike Toft, Mark Paisey and Bob Brownlow. Jack Calder and Bob Brownlow replaced the two Johns after they were shot down.

Gordon Buckley, who was awarded the DFC, and me on Christmas Day in the luxury of Bahrain.

*Above:* An American decoy plane on the tarmac at Tabuk, an airfield in Saudi Arabia.

*Right:* The entrance to the cramped ops block at Tabuk.

Tornadoes refuelling in mid-air from a VC10.

The final briefing before our first mission. Left to right: Gary, John Nichol, John Peters and me.

The two Johns photographed by me. This was the last picture taken of them before they were shot down.

Gary and me, after the ceasefire, sitting on a laser-guided bomb.

Nose art.

Debbie, my favourite jet, after the war. The bombs painted on the side indicate the number of missions flown. Pablo the Penguin was added after London Zoo named a penguin after me.

The body of a British serviceman being repatriated.

many times to take us to war and bring us home again, was in for routine maintenance. This time I would be flying Awesome Annie. And for our Buccaneer crews, bless them, who would be coming along to mark the targets for us, this was going to be their very first mission of the war. Apart from all that, we had everything on our side.

I was feeling bolshie at the time and felt like pointing out to the mission planners that the Tornado forces had not suffered a loss for around three weeks. Did they feel it was time to boost the publicity, by getting a couple of us shot down and the RAF back in the public eye again?

Gary and I pored over the targets and the intelligence that had already been collated. Then we desperately tried to work out a way in and a way out again for four Tornadoes and two entirely novice Buccaneer crews. We argued, considered the plans again, argued some more and at times got close to punching each other.

It was simply an almost impossible task: how the hell was I going to bring my boys out of that alive? Yet this was something I suppose we should have got used to. Gary and I had been the first at most things, including leading the way with laser-guided bombing. But this was not just an extremely difficult target; it was two extremely difficult targets in the same sortie.

Eventually we came up with a plan. We would almost certainly be under fire from close to reaching the first target until shortly after we left the second. Our lives had always become very interesting in the target area, where defences were at their highest. But that focus of our terror, although it always seemed as though we were transfixed for an age, lasted just seconds. They were seconds when our lives were thrown into a lottery. Our skill was of great value to us but in those few seconds luck ruled the game.

We had honed our approach to this sortie as finely as we could, but we could not escape the fact that we were almost certain to be under fire for at least ten minutes. How on earth was I going to manage to get six aircraft through that?

I briefed the mission, going over every detail with a fine toothcomb. No longer could I casually use the slogan SOP (Standard Operating Procedure) – all of my team, including the two I had lost on our first mission, fully understood the instruction. My team of eight were now into double mission figures, but we would be taking with us four wide-eyed aircrew who needed to drink in my every word. It was their very first war sortie and it was also one of the most complex missions of the entire war.

Just a few minutes after 6 a.m. local time we took off from Muharraq on yet another beautiful morning. The sun was already rising and the reds and pinks painted across the sky seemed so very cruel to me. How could the world be so lovely when any one of us may soon never see its beauty again? I just wondered how many of us would be there to see that sun set that night.

The early part of our mission ran on rails. We refuelled smoothly and no one reported any aircraft malfunctions. Two and a quarter hours after take-off we eased across the border from Saudi into Iraq. Moments after slipping into enemy territory there was an excited call on our closed radio of a SAM 2 missile at the three o'clock position. I tried to calm the worried young voice I didn't even recognize and strove to reassure him that it was probably a false alarm, since most of the enemy defences close to the Saudi border were now well asleep.

The next fifteen minutes were pretty quiet as we flew a zig and a zag; we flew north-easterly headings, north-westerly headings and finally turned in on our attack heading. I had only just turned in on our attacking track to the first enemy airfield when the excited chatter from the young Buccaneer crews began again. We had just begun our run in to the target and I was worried their nervous tension would cloud their concentration and ordered them to be quiet.

There was no doubt that these poor guys were suffering: this sortie was a hell of a challenge for my team and we had already been at war for weeks. We knew what Triple A looked like, and we had seen plenty of flak. We knew the smell of fear and the colour of adrenalin. Here were our new boys alongside us on one of the most complex missions. I was already dreading our fortunes.

With just a few seconds left to our bomb release over the first target, my Buccaneer called a problem and we overflew it. As we broke out to the left, Triple A opened up almost straight away. While most of it was going off below us, I rolled out on my heading to attack the second target, which now seemed an eternity away.

There was a good ten minutes to go when a missile arced harmlessly under the port wing and the Buccaneer boys began their near-hysterical chatter again. They had never seen anything like this before. The other Tornadoes followed me into the first target with varying degrees of success as the trailing Buccaneer did his best to mark the targets.

Our success at the first target was very limited and once more I had aimed to deliver two of my laser-guided bombs there, keeping one for the second leg of our mission. In the event, I was still carrying a full war load on board, with three bombs intact. We had to compose ourselves as best we could after that foul-up, since we had just a few minutes left to run in to the second target.

Approaching from the east it was easy to see that from the first attack the enemy had been warned of our impending arrival. The Triple A opened up at least a minute before we got overhead and we threaded our way through, just praying our number was not on any of their guns.

Much of the action was going on just below us but it was a damn sight closer than at the first airfield. I ran in and everything looked good and it sounded good over the radio. I released my bombs and started the stopwatch. I had a few seconds spare to take a look at the target area to see how well we had done.

We had been tasked against the hardened aircraft shelters on the airfield and as I looked down at where my bombs should have hit at the precise moment of impact, I could see I had completely missed. They had made three holes in the sand, well short of any shelters and only just inside the airfield perimeter.

I broke out to the south and we were on full throttle, trying to get just as high as we could, away from the range of enemy attack. I had gone all that way just to build three ornamental fish-ponds in the middle of the desert.

There was still too much to think about to get my boys home safe. We were weaving and diving and climbing, when we had the power, as we ran away south.

Gradually the smoke plumes of the missiles being thrown at us died off, along with the small grey and white and occasionally black puffs of Triple A.

As we were diving away south I listened intently on the radio for all the other excited gabbles from my team as missiles were called and break manoeuvres were flown. Triple A was called as the aircraft crews diverted to avoid its burst. I said nothing to any of them and just listened until, three or four minutes after the target, everyone called in safe. We had all just flown into a boiling cauldron and stayed there for ten minutes.

At our debrief we recommended that no such complex task should ever be given out again. As far as I am aware, that was the only task of the entire war where a formation was sent up against two airfields in one sortie.

Now the worst was surely over and we had an hour and a half before landing back at our base.

There was still nearly twenty minutes at full throttle to go before we crossed into the sanctuary of Saudi airspace. Just ten minutes before we finally made it, I painfully discovered that only one thing could be as terrible as losing my own wingman in battle. That had to be listening to someone else about to die.

Although we were still running south as fast as we could, the pressure had eased. Most of the hullabaloo was over now. We were picking up the radio calls from other teams going in to targets, when we picked up the calls from a team of Saudi fighter-bombers being led by an American.

We were only just short of going in to meet our own refuelling tankers when we picked them up. There was a call-sign, Hunter formation, and it sounded as though they were having a bit of a turkey-shoot. They were ground-attack jets and they had picked up some juicy target, a convoy of military vehicles. They were tearing the convoy to shreds slowly and methodically.

The Hunter formation was mostly being flown by Arabs and much of what they had to say on the radio I simply didn't understand. But then I suddenly heard a guy scream out, 'Hunter Two-Six, strobes on me.' It meant that his warning equipment had told him that there was a radar guiding either Triple A fire or SAM. The radar would have him full in its sights and would be firing.

There was a terrible, ear-piercing scream and then nothing. The Arabic gabble started up again and I picked out 'no chutes'. It was obvious the aircraft had gone down and the occupants had had no time to eject; there were no parachutes. It would have taken a full hit and simply tent-pegged into the ground. No one got out.

Then there was a pause as the whole of the airwaves became crystal clear. I will never forget the supreme calm in the voice of the formation's American leader. He must have known there were probably hundreds of us up there hanging on his every word. The guy sounded as laid-back as if he had just taken a stroll down a sunny Californian beach. He called out to his terrified team, 'OK guys, let's just get on and do the jaab we came to do.'

We all gave a quiet salute to their dead comrade before getting on with the business of war. It was all the time that anyone could have afforded him.

But that American was dealing with the fear of all his team. Shortly after his last order we could hear the calls continue as their remaining aircraft carried on engaging the target and diving in. I would like to meet that man some day.

I now know that I and my whole team had listened in to an airman's dying words: 'Hunter Two-Six, strobes on me.' I shall never forget them.

We crossed the border and refuelled on our way home and landed shortly after 10.30 a.m. I felt a bitterness inside, a mix of sorrow, sadness and then joy that I had just survived that complex and demanding sortie.

After our debrief I glanced at the programming board to see what was in store for us on our next mission the very next morning. On Thursday 14 February we were to be tasked against the first target of the previous day: that same horrible, heavily defended airfield at Al Taqaddam, forty miles west of Baghdad.

I went to bed very early and fell into a fitful and troubled sleep. We were going back into the burning cauldron again. In my sleep I ran through the terrifying images of that mission. There had been no real time during the sortie itself to reflect on how scared we had been. We had just eighteen hours left to plan the next attack and grab a few hours' sleep before going in. It had been three weeks since we had lost any Tornado aircrew and in my dreams I feared the worst.

It seemed to me that no matter how well we were doing, winning the war and achieving triumph after triumph, the powers that be, in their ivory towers or Portakabins, wherever they were, kept on asking for more.

The take-off on the next, our fourteenth, mission was planned for 6.01 a.m. This time I would be leading an incredible massed formation of twelve aircraft to attack the airfield. There were eight Tornadoes and four Buccaneers to guide us in. We all taxied down the runway to take off on time and flew straight into trouble.

There was considerable cloud cover and we had the added complication of refuelling at three separate tankers. In all, there would be fifteen aircraft in the same piece of sky trying to avoid collision. The radio was completely cluttered as we tried to split the formation up and tell each other where we were. In peacetime I know I would have been terrified and would probably have gone home. But we were at war and I couldn't see that we had any choice other than to carry on.

We were separated by just a few hundred feet as we headed west in three very tight groups of five. At one point I looked down briefly to see an American tanker with its four F16 aircraft in tow, pointing in the opposite direction and no more than a couple of hundred feet below us. That was not organization; it was just pot luck. And it was luck that we even had the grace of those two hundred feet to save us from collision.

Shortly after, we were crossing the border and flying our well-tested zigzag style of route towards the target. We would be reaching it in just twenty minutes along the one remotely safe lane through the heavy defences that would be waiting to greet us. We would all be attacking in one long trail and five minutes to the target I could already hear that the guys down the back were experiencing some excitement.

A SAM 2 missile arced close to the rear of the formation but I could hear that it had continued harmlessly back down towards the desert floor.

We turned into the target and concentrated all our efforts on releasing our bombs. This time the Buccaneer boys, with just one mission's experience, came up with the goods. They had learned their job quickly and this time they guided my bombs to perfection on to the target. They scored direct hits on the hardened aircraft shelters but there was no time to hang around to admire my handiwork.

I broke off left on a north-west heading to give me some safe distance from the aircraft running in right behind me. Then I turned south for home.

As I listened intently to the other aircraft running in I heard the calls: 'Two; three; four; five.' Everyone was doing well and the hardened aircraft shelters were taking a pounding from our bombs. The first half of the formation had all scored direct hits.

Then number seven, pilot Nigel Risdale and the squadron boss, seemed to be having problems. But their confidence was running so high that they decided to fly a race-track pattern and run in to the target once more. They were determined not to take their bombs home again.

My concentration was suddenly interrupted by a call from number twelve. The Buccaneer who was marking the target for the aircraft ahead of him screamed, 'Two missiles airborne and heading for the formation.'

Seconds later a sharp-eyed American on our escort shrieked, 'SAM, SAM, SAM.' He had seen that there was a missile off the rails and gunning for one of us. The next moment I saw two puffs of black smoke just off my port wing as I was running south and the last of our team was running north in to the target.

There was an explosion, just a beam of bright light, and I realized it had hit one of our aircraft. It was our number eleven crew, pilot Rupert Clark and navigator Steve Hicks.

Then I saw another SAM 3 missile explode on the other side of their jet, but I could see the aircraft was still intact as it came out of the second blast and was still flying. The only visible damage was a thin trail of smoke as it dived northwards. This looked strangely graceful as it died away back into enemy territory.

A couple of our guys tried desperately to raise the crew on the radio, urging them to eject. As we ran south we kept looking back, in the hope that we would see some sign to tell us they were out, and at least alive. But their jet plodded gently on its secluded path until it was out of sight. No one saw it hit the ground or anyone eject.

Their loss brought back all the terrible recriminations and self-doubt. The guilt flooded back as I questioned why it was that something had saved my life yet they were gone.

The boss and his pilot, Nigel Risdale, cancelled their re-attack and ran south with the rest of us.

It had been three weeks since the last aircraft loss and our tasking was still increasing. We were already measuring our success in terms of victory as daily we flew over hollow, burned-out shells that had once been heavily defended oil terminals and airfields.

But, the day before, we had flown a near-impossible mission and today we had flown a massed attack on the same airfield, which was probably already on its last legs.

Maybe the missile that had hit Rupert and Hicksey was just a lucky one, or unlucky for them, but how could we justify sending so many aircraft up together against one target that had already had its day?

We later discovered, at the end of the war, that poor Rupert, who had managed to safely eject, had been captured and very brutally beaten and tortured by the Iraqis. But Steve Hicks was killed as he sat in the jet.

Hicksey, I am really very sorry . . .

Within the first two weeks of the war it had been intimated from on high that some of the Tornado aircrew were perhaps displaying a lack of moral fibre. True, we had all requested a change in tactics from the low-level bombing missions of the very early days. This was not just because of the heavy losses we were so obviously suffering and would continue to suffer if we carried on with those suicidal tactics. It was also because of the terrible fear, constantly with all the aircrews, of becoming the next statistic.

There was also tremendous reluctance to deliver the JP233. This is a terrifying weapon to receive and to deliver. It contains hundreds of anti-personnel mines and several highly effective cratering devices. When it is delivered accurately, it would be possible to put the remains of an airfield runway through a colander.

In order to make an effective delivery over the target, invariably a runway, the jet must be flown straight and level, a couple of hundred feet above the runway surface, for well over fifteen seconds. This is exactly the time when all crews feel most vulnerable. All the airfield defences are on alert and you are forced to sit there waiting until all your munitions have been dropped on the target.

Many of us were ordered to deliver this devastating weapon during the early days of the conflict. I was lucky enough to miss out on taking the JP233 and it is something I will never regret. Those orders lasted for the first three days of the war, after which our tactics changed to delivering cast-iron and forged 1000-lb bombs. They were easier for aircraft manoeuvrability but nowhere near as effective. There is no other weapon like the JP233. Its powers of devastation are colossal and would paralyse an entire enemy target. The anti-personnel mines actually carried on exploding for hours after our boys had left the target area.

Aircrew Nigel Elsdon, Gary Lennox, Max Collier and Kev Weeks were all killed during JP233 missions. The deaths of these four were certainly tragic events for us, but opinion remains divided as to exactly what happened.

The official version is that the cause of death remains undetermined in each case. But there are those who believe that they flew into the ground either while attempting to deliver the JP233 or during the recovery from the attack; that they flew into the ground because they felt so vulnerable; that, in trying to hide from the enemy radars that could so easily pick them up, they tried desperately to hug the ground to avoid being spotted and simply flew right into the earth.

We were all reluctant to carry on delivering these lethal weapons. A few crews and individuals had already refused to go to war. Others were fast approaching breaking point. In the Second World War they would have been branded as lacking in moral fibre and would probably have lived a life of misery, shunned by their services comrades for the rest of their days. In the First

World War they would simply have been taken out and shot.

Thank God we have become more compassionate and sensible in our attitudes towards the people who were unable to make that final jump to war. Most of them, I know, are still in the Air Force and will carry on with a productive career although, quite naturally, it is unlikely that they will continue as fast-jet aircrew.

I was not sure at the time whether I possessed the real courage that these guys had. On many occasions I felt I lacked the courage to go on and yet I was more scared of making that advance towards telling my commanding officer. So, they would order me to go and I would carry on, mission after mission. It was far more stupid, really. You could say to someone that if these certain conditions exist, then I am not going to lead my boys on that mission. But I never did.

For quite a while I envied the people who were removed from theatre and sent back home. The system was such that you would see an aircrew one day and then they were gone or the pilot or navigator had another flyer sitting in the cockpit with him. Someone would ask a few questions but as soon as we were told he had gone back, that would be the end of it. No one wanted to know.

I had obeyed orders from the very outbreak of war, but now, more than a few missions later, what had I got to lose by admitting that I too couldn't go on? It would have been passed off as battle fatigue and I would have been excused from risking my life again.

I never did find the courage to refuse to go and

I carried on obeying orders. Sometimes they were stupid orders, but I still led my boys to war.

Since the end of the conflict I have met a couple of the blokes who said no. While I don't think I bear them any animosity, I found it very difficult to talk to them or relate to them. We could chat about very neutral subjects like cars or the poll tax, but the war was always studiously avoided.

At about 8 a.m. on 20 January my team was busily planning our next mission. But, as we sat around the ops room we knew that other guys from our own XV Squadron were due back. This team was led by pilot Nigel Risdale and the squadron boss, and all of us there were well aware that they had just flown their third JP233 mission in a row. We heard them arrive back and I looked up to greet their familiar faces.

Then I saw my friend. He was an empty shell and it seemed to me that he had difficulty in focusing on the rest of us who were there ready to welcome his safe return. I got up to go to him and I could sense that he radiated fear from every pore of his body. I didn't have to touch him to feel it and I tried, pathetically, to make light of his obvious deep-rooted distress by offering to make him a cup of coffee.

I had caught his eye as he stood, leaning for support against the wall of the corridor of the ops room. I just stared at him as he lit a cigarette and watched as his shaking hand had difficulty moving it to his lips.

I saw a chemical, rather than a simple physical change in my friend. Unlike water, which can be changed into ice and then back to water again, he had travelled through a door that was now locked

behind him and he could never pass back through
it again.

He had always smoked in a rather effeminate way,
holding the cigarette lightly between the tips of his
fingers. Now he cupped it tightly in his palm between
thumb and forefinger as he took a pull from it like a
miner who had just surfaced after a hard shift at the
coalface.

He spoke for no more than a minute and his first
words to me were a barely audible whisper. They
were meant only for me, his friend, and I knew he
meant it when he said, 'I'm never going to do that
again. That's it.'

I didn't believe myself when I answered that he
would be fine in the morning after a few beers and
a good night's sleep. It was absurd. I had not gone
as far down the same road as my friend, but even so
I was not sure whether, like him, I would find there
was nothing left to help me go again.

He was not asking for my help; he was simply
confiding in a trusted friend. He had already made
up his mind that he wanted to go home. What is
more, he was utterly determined that his next move
was to tell the powers that be that he would not be
flying again. If he had done that, I knew he would
never have flown fast jets for the RAF again.

To me, my friend showed a very special kind of
bravery. He had told me how scared he was flying
those three terrifying JP233 missions and he admitted
that he believed he had nothing left to give. His store
of courage had been emptied.

I realized that I had buried the same fears every

134

time I flew into war. But in reality I too wanted to go home, to be with my own family. I wanted to be safe and to stop running these endless crazy risks with my life. He had told me something I hadn't even dared to consider myself.

He didn't ask to be sent home, but flew eighteen more brave and demanding missions for the rest of the war. Somewhere he found the strength to continue his fight, or somebody else's fight, right to the end.

Since then we have never discussed what happened that day.

Very soon after we had lost Rupert and Hicksey on our fourteenth mission, I was sitting alone by the poolside bar at our hotel quarters, sipping a pint of bitter. I was alone with my thoughts of that last fateful mission, when one of the younger lads from another Tornado formation joined me. 'Hi, Dad, how's it going?' he called out, but I could tell just from the strain in his voice that the war was not going too well with him.

It was patently obvious that he didn't want to just pass the time of day with me; there was clearly something he needed to get off his chest. I tried hard to make him aware that I could sense there was something very wrong, so we chatted about the price of gold in the local market and about the weather. Then he just said it: 'It's no use, Dad, I just can't go on. I've flown fifteen missions and I want to go home.'

He took a deep gulp of breath and wiped his fingers over his cheeks, which were already glistening with tears. He waited for me to say something but I just sat quietly and continued looking at him. I knew there would be more for me to listen to and certainly it would be nothing that I could pass judgement on.

I felt relieved, perhaps because I too was feeling close to the edge. I had flown a similar number of missions and I dearly wanted to go home. But as a formation leader there was no one I could talk to. This young pilot interrupted my own thoughts as he carried on: 'I don't think I'm a coward. I've just had enough, that's all.'

I didn't think he was a coward either. I thought he was a very brave young man who had plenty of life ahead of him and certainly deserved a shot at it. He had put into words exactly the thoughts that were running through my own mind, and they had been with me for some time.

He talked for most of that evening and I just sat and listened to his every word. He was unburdening himself on me and I was making my contribution simply by being there. Gradually, his speech became a little more confident and more positive as he openly talked of his fears. He told me he daren't confide in his navigator because he didn't know if he was just as scared and he didn't want to shake his confidence any further. He had sensed his navigator's fear and it was something they had both very carefully avoided, as though they were frightened of fear itself.

I considered the parity between myself and my own navigator, Gary. We had never confided to each other our fears for our own safety or that of our team. As close as we had become, this had always been something of a no-go area for us too.

Now my young colleague had finished. He had said all he wanted to say and he looked a little brighter. As he got up to leave me, he said, 'Thanks, Dad, thanks for being there and thanks for helping me to deal with my fear.' I reassured him that any time he needed to chat he could do so in absolute confidence.

He had unburdened himself, but in doing so he had placed an extra burden on my shoulders. Had I now got to take his fears into battle along with my own? I honestly don't believe I ever did. For me, his admission came as a relief. I had allowed him to believe that he was doing the right thing by deciding to carry on. Now I had to carry on too, regardless of the fears and terrible misgivings that were rumbling around in my thoughts.

As he went off to get some rest, I didn't doubt that he would be there alongside the rest of us, ready to take his place on the next battle mission. But he left me that evening having just accorded me the wisdom of the apostles.

Fear was my constant companion throughout the war, but its nature did change. I could see there was a huge difference between the emotions I was experiencing and those of, say, a parachutist, a rock climber or even a test pilot.

In the early days of the war there was a kind of competition running, a league where you had to fly as many sorties as the next man. It was the only way we could share an understanding as equals in this war. When we came back from our very first taste of battle my team were very different men from the crews who had not yet flown to war. We had been blooded, but we had also been very afraid.

Perhaps that first mission had been worse for us because we had lost a crew. When the guys climbed into the cockpit for the second and then the third time, their fears had built up to a climax. The first time, it had been exciting and a new and thrilling experience. Then the fear would build up each time they went off to war. By the third mission we were all beginning to realize it was a lottery, with the odds against us.

In a way the build-up of fear was like an electric charge, like having an accumulator inside you. If there was a way in which we could run this charge back into the earth then there would be room for more fear. We found many ways to run our batteries to earth, often without really looking for them: a few drinks too many one night, a rowdy singsong at the bar or a noisy game of snooker with the whole team crowded around the table. But one of the most rewarding ways was to have a success over the target. The joy that would often come over the radio from a triumphant crew was always incredible.

I always found it difficult to express my jubilation or even frustration over the airwaves but I was always encouraged to hear at first hand over the radio words like: 'Good shot, Steve, see that baby burn.'

Sometimes I would hear the same cries a few hours later, after a mission was complete, as we gathered for a drink at the bar. You could hear the repeated exploits of a young man who wanted to tell the world just how bloody well he had done.

Perhaps, though, he had gone a little too far. He had

told us how he had got to get into that target at all cost; he had got to hit that oil cracking tower or hardened aircraft shelter. I suppose it was target fixation.

It had also happened among crews in peacetime. On big exercises there would be foolhardy exploits with fatal results. There are well-documented cases in previous wars of bombers, for no apparent reason, just flying straight into the target.

Maybe the pilot was reaching his total accumulation of fear and just had to dispel it at that moment. One guaranteed way to run that fear to earth is to score a solid hit on the target; to make the others whoop for joy as the internal battery becomes totally drained again and makes room for more fear in the future.

Of course, each one of us had to deal with his own misgivings in his own way. As the leader of my own formation, I could not be seen to be weak or reluctant to fly the next mission. What effect would that have had on the rest of my team? I had to take my fears with me back into the air. I didn't actually see it as a burden because I had been elected to lead my boys into battle. So I was stronger, and maybe I needed to absorb their fears as well. Somewhere I knew I must suppress my desires to go home, to get out of a war that was none of my causing.

My boys always called me Dad, and this was as important to me as it was to them. I wanted to feel that I was part of a family and head of that family. I certainly did not want to be a tyrannical father. I preferred to be one who nurtured and encouraged his family to have trust in themselves, in their own judgement. It was therefore inevitable, because of my unique style of leadership, that on occasion my boys should overstep the mark. At times I too would overstep the mark, by being too liberal.

Sometimes we would have minor tiffs and clear the air, but at other times the atmosphere would build up until I stepped in to sort out a minor problem that had developed.

During the planning stages of a mission I adopted a different approach from that of all the other formation leaders. There were guys in my formation who were better than others during the planning stage and I allowed them all to fully hone their individual skills. Within the overall plan we developed a set of tasks which each member of the team knew he had to perform.

Once Gary and I had agreed the outline of our task, he would get on with the meticulous planning. And Bob, our weapons instructor, would analyse the target and the weapons we were carrying. He would calculate fuse settings, perhaps suggesting that we may need to alter our attack direction in order to get better effects, better collateral damage from a stick of bombs.

Jack Calder, the master of the one-line quip, but also our expert on complex calculations, made sure that the detailed computer tapes we fed into the Tornado's computer had the correct information. 'Garbage in, garbage out', as computer programmers say, was not going to be our problem out there.

Chris Lunt would always prepare the briefing sheet we took with us to war: a simple sheet of white paper full of all sorts of coded information we all understood. His handwriting was always meticulous; it almost looked as though he had prepared the brief on a typewriter.

Colin Ayton, Stroppy Jock, was our master tanker planner and he would talk at length to the refuelling tanker crews, telling them precisely where they should be and when. He would also tell us exactly how much fuel we would need to take on each uplift.

Mark Paisey, Mr Pastry, was our general dogsbody; a jack of all trades and master of many.

Then there was Mike Toft, Tofty, who would help Gary with the fuel and wind calculations.

That left me. It would have been very easy for me to have become far more involved in the planning stages, but it would have been just as easy for me to have had an intricate knowledge of just one small aspect of our plan. I couldn't do that, since I needed to have an overview of everything, and it saved our bacon a couple of times.

I often looked over someone's shoulder to see how he was working and then over another boy's shoulder, and I could instantly spot a conflict in our plan. Also, I often wandered around the various intelligence departments within the ops building while my boys were planning, to see if I could rustle up some extra support from outside. We had, on an earlier mission, vowed never to rely on Allied support again. But certainly there was nothing wrong with adopting a belt-and-braces approach.

My style, though, did create an element of friction within the team because the boys would be working like one-armed paper-hangers to produce their own small contribution to the broader task. I would stand there, apparently just trying to monitor their general progress and not really appearing to do much at all. Often I would go out to the drinks cooler and bring in a tray of soft drinks for my boys.

At times I would look around at others who were team planning. There would be the formation leader, at the hub of things, throwing out his orders and issuing his instructions. The boys would be running around, sometimes vanishing up their own backsides as tasks were duplicated, triplicated and, more often than not, more complicated than was ever really necessary.

That wasn't my style. I would never be right in the middle of the planning because there was always the possibility that, as I took a focal interest in one aspect, something else would fall over the side and not be noticed until it was too late. I had to be able to see as much or as little as I wanted at any one time.

Where I know I definitely let myself and my boys down was in the briefing stage. What I should have done was gather the information we had well before the briefing, so that I was better prepared. What I was doing when I stood out there in front of them was trying to find out for myself precisely what was going to happen. On occasion, I would ask them questions about what we were expected to do. They often knew more than I did. I was wrong. I also know I would do a better job next time.

Where the boys felt I had let them down more than anything was when we, as a team, were leading an even larger formation. My lads were well aware of my foibles and my inadequacies. But I think I embarrassed them once or twice when I was briefing a massed formation and I gave the impression that I didn't know precisely what was going on. Of course, up until the briefing stage I didn't know what was going on. I had sat aside and let them get on with it. But I admit now that I should have been better prepared.

There were many clashes with my team, mostly trivial and invariably dealt with in an instant or over a pint or two of beer. Because I had laid down the rules, there were to be no secrets, nothing to be bottled up.

Yet after that fateful mission on 14 February, when we lost Rupert and Hicksey, we finished the debrief and at the end I asked all but my own team to leave. The boss's team left and our Buccaneer mates left with them. In the end there were eight of us standing in the room together. It was obvious that the friction between us had built up quite dramatically. In fact, I had let it go for a few days because the team was performing well. But it was almost as though they were ganging up against me, seven against one.

For a couple of our recent missions I had been happy with this because they were integral, intact. But I also felt they were treating me as an outsider. I knew that this was almost certainly because of my attitude during the planning stage and I decided it was time to knock it on the head.

During the outbound leg of the last mission we had plugged into the refuelling tanker. One thing we did as a matter of course was to switch off our anti-collision lights when we were about to manoeuvre into position behind a refuelling hose. This let everyone know, without cluttering the radio waves, that one of us was manoeuvring into position.

I watched Bob Brownlow, my faithful number two, manoeuvre his jet into position, but he still had his anti-collision lights flashing. I simply transmitted: 'anti-colliders' and in return received a stream of verbal abuse over the radio. It was obvious that he was on a very short fuse. But I was determined that something should be done at the end of the sortie to either light that fuse and cause an explosion or to dampen it down again.

At the end of the debrief I stood in front of my boys and I said I understood that there were advantages and disadvantages to my style of leadership. The advantage of course was that everyone had a say, some input to our own destinies, collective and individual. I wasn't about to stamp on these blokes unless it was absolutely necessary, but now it seemed it had become necessary.

I stared Bob Brownlow full in the face and warned him that if ever he spoke to me again like that, either over the radio or in person, then I would take his testicles and wear them for a pair of braces.

I can't remember how long my speech was, but at the end I was very lucid. I was determined to show them that I was in charge and, while we allowed committee decisions on everything, whatever the committee decided, I would be entirely responsible for.

Bob remained silent for a moment and then he apologized to me for his rudeness. It was a great weight off my mind and I too apologized to him and my team for perhaps having let them down by my seemingly casual approach to them during our previous missions.

The air was already becoming much clearer and then Lunty said, 'Pablo, d'you know, on occasions you really are a right prat, but there's no one else I'd rather fly with.'

He really did give me the boost I needed, because I was feeling very down at the time, and almost a total outsider from my team.

Gary said nothing, as usual; he rarely said anything at all during the debrief and I often wondered why.

It felt to me as though each one of us during the previous weeks had built up his own reservoir of feelings, of fear, and possibly disillusionment. Some of us perhaps felt more down than others at that moment but there we all were, sounding off and putting all our emotions into the same big pool. In the end we all jumped into that pool and we took out the same amount of emotion. It was a relief because I think that those who had a little bit of spare capacity put it into the pool and those who were running out took extra from the pool. But I am also convinced that when we left that debrief we were all at the same emotional level again.

When my style of leadership had been questioned during the war, I prostrated myself in front of my team. I asked them what they would like to change and, more importantly, whether they wanted to leave me and fly with someone else. If anyone had said yes I would have done all I could to assist his move. But

I knew at the end of that debrief that there was no one in that room who didn't want to fly with me or who would rather fly with anyone other than those present. I was very grateful for what happened; it was the most momentous occasion for me in the whole war.

Now it was time to leave our base and head back to the Sheraton Hotel for a bit of solitude and reflection. I had to accept that, because of my particular style of leadership, I had very nearly lost complete control. But as I pulled on those reins again, my team came right back to me; they had fully accepted that I was the boss.

The programming board showed that we wouldn't be flying the following day, so those who wanted to could go and tie one on at the hotel bar. I spent quite a few hours alone in my room that day before making my way to join the others down at the bar. There was plenty of time to decide what to do with the evening, now that my lifespan was extended to at least another full day.

We considered ourselves fortunate because our base at Muharraq had a pretty good relationship with the television and newspaper reporters who were covering our part in the war for the folks back home. They even shared the same luxury hotel accommodation and we became good friends and close confidants with many of them. And there was certainly nothing either the RAF or the press boys could teach each other about the art of serious drinking!

After I had showered and changed, I made my way to the poolside bar, and spotted another formation leader, Gordon Buckley, chatting to TV-AM's reporter Tony Birtley. It suddenly occurred to me that our lost pilot, Rupert Clark, had planned a game of squash with Tony later that day. I could see that Tony had no idea about Rupert and Hicksey's fate earlier that morning. As soon as the two guys saw me, Gordon called out a cheery greeting. All I could find to say was simply, 'Tony, I am very sorry, we lost your squash partner today . . .'

He reacted as I knew he probably would: there was utter disappointment and a shared look of fear in his eyes. Like many of the media guys, he had grown to share our feelings. They became almost an integral part of our lives, and some of them were closer to us than even the operations staff or the ground crew.

Of course, many ground rules had to be laid down. Firstly, we had our families to think about. And we had our own lives to consider if, as did happen early on, some vital aspect of our mission was flashed around the world on television while we were taxiing down the runway on our way to battle.

Once war actually broke out, strict rules were laid down by the station boss, Group Captain David Henderson. But he also took a very sensible approach by allowing the aircrews to decide for themselves if they wanted to speak to the press about their previous missions.

Initially there were three groups of aircrews: those who wanted to speak to the press, those who definitely did not and those who didn't mind. At first I was one of the definitely 'did nots'. I had very mixed feelings about journalists and the way they operate to get hold of a story. It stemmed from my experiences as a helicopter pilot and the way that many of the facts about the success or failure of an air-sea rescue mission were misreported.

My trust was very low and I simply did not want to get involved in giving my story. However, I became increasingly disappointed and then angry about the way the aircrew interviewing was going and about the gung-ho comments that were being made by some of the younger guys about those early missions.

I regularly spoke to many of the guys, not just the boys in my team, just after they returned from a bombing mission. I had seen the fear in their eyes, in their voices and in their very demeanour. Yet only half an hour later they would be led out by some duty officer to be interviewed in front of the TV cameras.

Then you would hear them trot out how it was 'all in a day's work, really rather good fun'. I really hated that and so did many of us. I decided I wanted to put my side of the story as I saw it then and as I still see it now. Yes, there was great joy in hitting a target and there were always beaming smiles when we came home that would indicate the total success of the sortie.

But there was also the sorrow and fear and terrible anguish that we needed to tell to the folks back home. Perhaps if they could understand that for most of the time it was bloody awful and a shocking waste, then maybe that was one of the ways we could stop this sort of carnage happening again. Hopefully, as the world struggles to become a more civilized place, it won't happen again.

What I really despised about all the media attention

was the pressure that was put on some of the younger guys by our leaders to almost tell the public what it wanted to hear rather than tell it as it really was.

There was positive censorship too. The bosses would protect many of the guys who climbed out of the cockpit after a night bombing raid over Baghdad because they were visibly shaking from their horrific experiences. These guys, often crying pitifully, were shepherded away from the glare of the camera lights just in case they blew the lid off this whole charade and showed their emotions to the world.

I spoke to my team very early on and told them I was happy for them to do any press interviews. But one thing I insisted on was that they had to tell it like it was and how they had seen it, not as the people back home wanted to hear it.

I believe I told it like it was, too. And for those people who are still prepared to listen I will certainly tell them how it was. Almost nothing has changed my views about the Gulf War. I am not ashamed to say now that I was scared and I was never ashamed to say that I was scared then.

One of my men once confessed to me that if I was unable to fly out to war, then he would not be able to go either. He frankly admitted that he would fix his machine to make sure that it was unserviceable for flying. I don't know whether he really meant what he said and I hoped that, if for some reason I was unable to fly, he would do his duty regardless.

I still like to think that my team were able to take strength from each other as well as from me. But I also hope that they could think and act as individuals, displaying their own personal bravery.

Maybe I was this particular lad's personal lucky charm. If I was there, he was going to be there. Perhaps he had spotted some weakness or despondency in my outlook and it was his way of chivvying me along. Whatever it was, his confession became a particular burden to me, yet another responsibility, but I became grateful for it. If, for some reason, I lost the edge and turned to run for home, then someone else would also be running with me. Not because he was scared, but because I was going.

I wanted the men to trust me. I wanted them to come to war with me. But I didn't see that it was wrong that they should know I was scared too. Perhaps some of the other formation leaders felt that I should have been more like them. They put up an indomitable shield to prove they had true grit, show that they weren't scared. Maybe they weren't scared.

But I know that I echo the views of many men who were out there with me. There were guys from the Tornado forces who went to war and admitted that they had been scared, terrified.

And there were also the liars.

# 5

# Disillusionment

Throughout the war and up until this day, I have never received any formal information on the success or otherwise of our very first attack on that Iraqi airfield, in which we lost the two Johns.

Ironically, the only report of our handiwork came from the Iraqis. Months later I spoke to John Peters again for the first time since he had been released and had returned to our base at RAF Laarbruch. He told me how the Iraqis had revealed to him the devastating success of our first sortie. During one of many very harsh interrogations, his Iraqi captors told him that our team had made a good job of the airfield.

It seems that all had not been lost, but our success both that time and on other missions did nothing to help the grim treatment that our prisoners of war received from brutal Iraqi guards. For some, it is certain that our work only made their position even worse. They all surely suffered dreadfully. I cannot imagine, from the many conversations we have subsequently had, that they can have any positive thoughts about a foreign war that very nearly cost their lives.

For myself, I am not sure how or why a sinking feeling of pointlessness about my whole purpose in the war began to creep into my thoughts. That sense of disillusionment was never there during the early days of the conflict. But it certainly built up as I moved beyond the anger and sorrow that two of my dear friends had been shot down, and beyond the excitement of that first mission.

It was only three days after the two Johns had been hit that we all heard they were safe. They had been seen on TV, bruised, bloodied and bowed but alive. For all of us, it was a wonderful contrast to the dejection we had all suffered at their loss.

Our very next bombing mission, on 20 January, against an incredibly well-defended airfield, had left us riding high on our success.

The two Johns had only just been replaced by new wingmen Bob Brownlow and Jack Calder. Those new guys had arrived from their base at RAF Bruggen in West Germany the day before. They turned up at our hotel quarters each clutching only a tiny holdall with their belongings for the entire war. Just nineteen hours later they were preparing to fly to war.

We called them Jack and Jill, probably because they arrived as a ready-made pair. Jack always had a ready smile and an impish sense of humour. He could look at the most demanding target, with what seemed to be almost impenetrable defences. Then he would smile at me and Gary as we were trying to fathom a way of getting in. He would regularly offer encouragement by saying, 'Looks like a piece of old doddle to me, Dad. You won't be needing my advice.'

Then he would wander off singing. His great skill was to lift so much of the burden of worry from my shoulders.

We were already experiencing a new euphoria over our recent successes, as well as relief that we were now all regularly getting home in one piece.

After we returned from our first, fateful mission, if someone had said I could pack up and go home I would have gladly done so. But two days later I would have gladly punched that same person in the face for making such an outrageous suggestion. There was no way I was going home when we were doing so bloody marvellously.

I could now understand the overwhelming joy of other crews who had gone out and all come back again. I had earlier stood aside, finding it hard to accept their throwaway lines like 'It ran on rails' or 'Have they surrendered yet?' But now we had just come home from a magnificent sortie and we were all raring to go again.

I recall telling a TV reporter who had been waiting to talk to us at the foot of our Tornado's steps that it had gone well. There had been heavy flak, much heavier than before, but our success had not been tarnished by the loss of a comrade. We had taken eight out and brought them all back and I wanted the world to know how good that felt. How sad we had been the last time, but how much better the future seemed from here. I was on cloud nine and it showed.

I had no idea that my words, which were flashed around the world on television that day, had so much impact within the RAF. Months later I stumbled upon a document that I certainly was not entitled to read. It was written about me by my squadron commander, who had noted how I had been taken off missions for a couple of days because of the 'perceived' emotional turmoil I was in as a result of the losses incurred on the first sortie.

I certainly had not been aware that I had been taken off operations. As far as I was concerned, my flying programme was running normally. My mission plan during those early days had been well programmed. If, as this internal note claimed, I had been taken off operations, it must have been done so discreetly that I didn't even notice! If my emotional state had become so unreliable, why then had I been tasked on 20 January to lead eight aircraft into battle against an airfield target? Why on earth was I also programmed the following night to lead sixteen aircraft into another heavily defended airfield?

I have absolutely no regrets for showing to the world my distress at having lost two comrades, two very dear friends. The fact that I felt emotional and showed it didn't make me any less of a man. When it was time to go into battle again I was well prepared to do my job. I led with the same style that I led every single mission of the war.

I am sorry if that is not the way the RAF would like the bravery and courage of its men to be shown. I wanted others to understand a little, perhaps even appreciate a little, what it was really like.

There were many times when we would return, shaking from the heady cocktail of excitement, triumph and fear, with no time to reflect on the risks we had just taken.

We had returned in victory on 20 January. Less than twenty-two hours after landing, we were off again on the following night.

All of us had developed those extra skills that contributed so much to individual and team preservation. We had grown eyes in the backs of our heads, learned to pick up the different sounds of missiles and munitions aimed at us. We were skilful at detecting their position: ahead of us, behind our tails or, far more deadly, snaking their way up under our wings.

That night we were tasked to attack an airfield eighty miles west of Basra, Iraq's second biggest city. I would be leading sixteen jets, including eight who would join us from their base at Dahran, in Saudi Arabia. The plan would be as simple as possible. Gary and I agreed that we would adopt the tried-and-tested KISS principle: Keep It Simple, Stupid. After a brief telephone call to the RAF base at Dahran, we agreed to make separate plans for each team. They would come in behind us along their own track and the deconfliction between aircraft in the area would be sorted out with good timing.

Our old pals, the American AWACS boys, kept a good watch on the sky as they shepherded us in to our target and reported a 'clean picture'. It was a main Iraqi airforce operating base and it was known to be very heavily defended by Triple A and

SAMs. The airfield had already been attacked on several occasions in previous days, but Iraqi aircraft activity was still being reported, and this had begun to unsettle all of us. During the early days of the war they had managed to get virtually nothing off the ground in a bid to engage us in a dogfight.

But this had also troubled us. It was hard for us to believe that the Iraqis had just laid down and died. We couldn't believe this, at the time. Privately, we all prepared for what the Iraqis might do. Perhaps they were planning to launch one massed attack to achieve a huge military coup by destroying us in one raid. Were we to be the victims of such an onslaught of overwhelming odds?

Our fear was that we simply didn't know the answer. We had seen so little Iraqi air activity and we had also heard very little of them. Our own confidence, however, was always shored up by the support from our allies. Tonight, we were escorted by American Phantoms and F15 Eagle fighters. They could turn on a sixpence and they were out to do their damnedest to look after us.

If the mission was to be a success, our sixteen aircraft would have to deliver 128,000lb of high explosives on that airfield – almost sixty-four tons. Surely, if the Iraqis had any fight left in them by the beginning of that evening, they would have none left by the time we had completed the job we came to do.

We would be running a long way west along Saudi airspace and then eventually skirting off to the north. We planned to cross into Iraqi airspace to attack this airfield from the west, in the hope that it was a direction from which they would not expect us to attack.

Our aircraft would run through to the target as close together as we dared during the blanket of night. We couldn't see each other in the dark, but we also wanted to spend as little time as we could using our radars to paint the sky ahead. Our electronic activity would easily alert enemy sensors to our presence.

During our briefing I had pressed home the message that if our plan was flown precisely and to the split second, we could all be in and out of that target in a very short time. If the plan was confused by microseconds, the results could have been devastating. Two aircraft just touching wing-tips for a moment with so much fuel and munitions on board, would have ignited into a massive firework display.

If we went in too close, there was also the risk of dropping our bombs into someone else's face. If we staggered the jets too much, the tail-end charlies would have taken the full force from any enemy response.

With our briefing and final checks complete, we took off at 6.30 p.m. Our target was just over two and a quarter hours away and would involve two refuelling slots.

We slipped over the border into enemy territory on track and on time, thanks to good old Gary. As we passed across the boundary line we spoke briefly to our American Phantom and Eagle support, using our call-sign Newport. On every mission we carried the name of a British town or county.

It was another clear night but there was mist reported over the target area. If the Iraqis believed that shroud offered them any comfort, they were to be rudely disabused of that notion at precisely 8.48 p.m.

On the way in we even saw a whole convoy of military lorries moving towards our airfield target. They all had their headlights on and were totally oblivious to our presence.

Greig Thompson and his team made up our back four from Muharraq. I have no idea who was flying in the eight-ship formation that joined us from Dahran. Soon after we had crossed into enemy airspace, Greig's number two, Crusty Cobb, reported a severe kit malfunction. He had no choice but to turn for home. But he was determined not to take his bombs home and just ten miles inside Iraq he spotted a juicy-looking target and dived straight in, delivering all 8000lb of bombs. We learned all about his exploits later that night in the bar. He had clearly enjoyed himself offloading his luggage.

At the time we believed that targets of opportunity like this were fair game. It was not until after the war that we discovered they had been excluded from the start. At least Crusty had had his moment of glory.

Within minutes of entering enemy airspace some of my crew radioed indications that they had been 'locked up' by Iraqi fighters. From our own highly sensitive system we could see that enemy Fulcrum fighters and Mirage jets had us on their radar systems.

It took split-second timing for the whole formation to react by manoeuvring fast to break their lock on us. We could see they were tracking us ready for attack but we used that to calculate how to lose them. My eyes began to hurt as I concentrated on looking out for anything that could be chasing us. If there was a missile, we would need the finest judgement to pull hard away from it, just hoping the jet would hold together.

On many of our sorties we carried missile decoys in the hope that the enemy weapons would be tricked into chasing them and not us.

But the Iraqis also had SMART missiles and we knew we could not fool them. They can quickly realize they are chasing a decoy and will change direction to come after the real target.

We were not actually engaged by enemy aircraft, but it had been a tense five minutes. We pressed on into the target and the Iraqi defences began to open up only after our first bombs impacted. Over the target area, the Triple A was very heavy and we were getting both tracer and airburst fire coming up to meet us. Occasionally the odd rattle of fire came close and then a barrage of SAMs must have been launched in one go.

The tracer bullets, painted with phosphorus, glow white-hot even in broad daylight. They literally trace a path through the sky. Airburst consists of much heavier shells, fired from an AA gun. The shells do not explode until they reach a predetermined height or, with a radar fuse, explode near to something solid.

This rocketry, which could have been fired with precision, was now flying off in all directions, posing no real threat. It seemed that they had put on this very expensive firework display for our benefit. Perhaps even Allah couldn't manage to help guide their bombs into our path.

I turned away from the target and began our run on a south-westerly heading before turning south. We had time now as Gary ran the stopwatch down and called impact, and we dropped a wing to see what was happening on the target.

We had put four aircraft over one end of the airfield to hit the hardened shelters and four aircraft at the other. Any dispersion of bombs would then have maximum effect between the two ends of the airfield over the main runways.

Once again, the picture we saw was a testimony to our success. Shock circles of brilliant reds and orange radiated out, with the occasional extra burst of colour as a bomb blasted into a fuel bowser or an aircraft. The two main points of impact were pounded by our bombs as the radiating circles of fire finally met and overlapped.

As we ran from the target we all kept looking back at the explosive display still going on behind us. And as we raced out at 600mph we could still see the amazing sight of a white explosion turning slowly to blood-red. It was difficult to conceive that something so visually beautiful was causing so much destruction. You could have got a double-decker bus into each hole made by our bombs.

Then I was brought back to reality with a sickening

jolt as my jet began to rattle and clatter as though it was being shaken. More tracer was coming up to meet us and I was convinced we had been hit. But the instrumentation was still reading normal and Gary and I said nothing. Some of our boys were getting twitchy and I could hear calls that they were jettisoning underwing tanks and bomb carriers so they could get out quickly.

We had got through to the target and now we were heading back into Saudi airspace. Only four of the seven aircraft heading back to Muharraq stayed behind to refuel. As we joined up with our tankers and took up enough fuel to get home, one of the pilots asked if we were the last out.

It wasn't until we finally got home to our debrief that I met up again with those tanker crews. I discovered that they had been dismayed because they believed that we had lost four jets on that mission. They had refuelled eight on the way in and I had as good as told them that we four were the only ones to come back. I never made that mistake again; I made sure from then on to report the good *and* the bad news.

Yet again, it had run on rails. But there was more excitement ahead as we came home to land in the face of a full missile alert.

We had flown into Muharraq in the safe lane, which would help identify us as friendly aircraft. There was always the chance of being shot down by our own air defences if we carelessly strayed out of bounds. Our undercarriage was already lowered as we made our final approach in to land. The airfield was lit up and the lights radiated out to the surrounding town and sprawling Arab villages.

Then all hell broke loose as I heard 'Missile Alert, Missile Alert' burst out over the airwaves. I put on full power and cleaned the aircraft up as we climbed to 2000ft.

A Scud missile attack had been called and its destination, heading south, was still unknown. Muharraq was no longer our safe haven. I feared we were about to witness the same sort of devastation as that we had just inflicted.

Our immediate concern was for our own fuel levels. We had planned to get back into Muharraq on minimums, with nothing to spare. Luckily, our tankers were following us home and they managed to set up a race-track pattern over each end of the airfield from the centre lines of the runways out to sea. Within minutes we had taken enough fuel to keep us airborne and then we heard the all-clear.

As we landed and taxied in to our stands, we could see the ground crew still patiently waiting, ignoring all missile attack warnings, until we had come safely home.

On the night of 28 January Gary and I took a back-seat ride along with the rest of our four-ship formation. We joined as the rear element of a ten-aircraft attack on a petrol refinery 120 miles south-east of Baghdad. The attack was led by Nigel Risdale and the boss and I sat back to watch how another team was led.

We planned to attack along a line of oil cracking

towers, but minutes before take-off one guy, Steve Barnes, reported electronics failure. There was no way that Barnesey and his navigator Mike Barley were going to be left behind. They dumped their failed jet and clambered into a spare aircraft and caught up with us all a few minutes later. They must have done the 100-yard sprint and completed pre-take-off checks in record time!

We had problems that night from severe turbulence as we linked up to our tankers for fuel. All anyone heard as jets were weaving in and out around the Victor was someone whispering 'Close one' over the radio.

As the month progressed, the moon had got fuller and higher. I was relieved to be flying this medium-level attack in darkness, although it seemed almost like daylight.

It was obvious that the target defences were becoming much weaker as we all concentrated on scoring a full hit. Number three in the formation, Gordon Buckley, gave us all a running commentary on the success of our bombs. It was as though we were present at a darts match, waiting for Gordon to give his pronouncement on our scores. As a stick of bombs hit a juicy target he might have been a well-known television voice calling out, 'One hundred and eighty! A Triple Top!' We all heard him call out, 'Good shot, Barnesey. Well done, Cocky Rill.'

It was Gordon's way of chivvying on his team. There were whoops of delight as secondary explosions went off beneath us. Refineries were our favourite targets. If you scored a hit they looked spectacular, and I could often feel the heave under my jet as something really big went up.

That oil refinery burned for only two days but it had been well worth the visit.

On our way out we discovered our American escorts were clearly enjoying the fun. I heard a beautiful southern drawl call 'Good jaab' as a huge piece of refinery equipment came up to meet us.

As January rolled into February I began to question more and more what we were doing. There was no way we could continue operating at such an intensity. I knew that at some stage battle fatigue would become a problem. I'd already lost half a stone during the first week of war and I noticed that many of my comrades were much thinner. We could now measure our capacity to keep up the level of bombing raids in days rather than weeks.

My whole life hinged on the success of the previous sortie; I was only as good as my last job. If the last sortie had somehow failed, the tension would then reach breaking point before the next mission.

No one could eat a thing before we went out, but after a successful raid I could easily devour two steaks when we got home.

The rest of the world was also becoming absolutely convinced that Saddam Hussein had been thrashed, vanquished and not just beaten. But the pressure on us was still building. We just had to get more out of each day, each sortie. The missions were becoming more daring, more complex, more demanding. Most of our efforts during January had been flown at night when we couldn't see what was happening below us. Into February and on daylight missions, we could see for ourselves the precision results of the Bull's-eye War.

There were burning oilfields, burning petrol refineries and then our laser bombs crushed their bridges, airfields and runways. It was a precise and almost clinical scene. We had also hit towns and villages, but they were hardly scratched by comparison to what we had done to Saddam's military machine.

It became no longer vital for us to rely on dedicated fighter support from the Americans. They had simply carved Iraqi airspace up into grid squares and were now operating on a freelance basis. They could position their fighters anywhere they wanted, for the Iraqis had no defence to offer.

But were we playing a statistical game by sending our aircraft off again and again to bomb targets that clearly had no further tactical significance? Our enemy did not have a fight left, if they ever intended one from the outset.

I can recall an airfield attack which we flew on a very sunny Saturday morning. It was a laser mission on 23 February, flown by my four-ship with two Buccaneer mates with Tony Lunnon-Wood at the rear. The Bucks had even begun delivering their own bombs as well as spiking the targets for us. Once our attack was complete they would go in and carry out their own attack.

Our call-sign for this mission was 'AVON' and I can remember that as Tony went into a steep dive on to his target he delivered his bombs and called, 'Bang, bang, AVON calling.' We all cheered.

But that airfield remained as quiet as the grave. I felt like buzzing their control tower just to let them know we had arrived.

As we flew home we could see the whole country was on fire. Through the breaks in the thick, black clouds of smoke and fumes, we could see that what was once military hardware had become just piles of scrap metal for hundreds of miles around.

In the early days of the war I had joined in the challenge with other teams to fly the most missions, the most hours and then the most day and night sorties. But as our battle missions moved into double figures I lost interest, along with many other guys. We'd proved our bravery, our willingness to fight, but now many of us had begun to feel that we were working ourselves harder than was necessary. I made no attempt to influence whatever was programmed for my team. But there were those who were senior to me who could, and regularly did, jockey to fly particular sorties.

There were some who were dying to fly the most missions, the most hours. My squadron commander flew more missions than anyone else at Muharraq. For that I consider him a very brave man. I was told by a comrade that another formation had come very close behind him in mission numbers. He had grounded that formation to make certain that his outstanding mission figures stayed well ahead of anyone else's. If what my comrade reported is true, then my boss was not only brave – he was also stupid and arrogant.

Early on in the war, when our losses from Muharraq were high, we heard about a delightful little scheme to boost team morale. Some bright spark, sitting in his office, had decided to set us a little competition. Anyone who managed to fly more than twenty-four missions was guaranteed an all-expenses-paid weekend in the south of Saudi; out of the battle zone at some beautiful coastal resort hotel. It did not take a genius to work out that if we continued to sustain the losses of those early days then there would not be enough of us left to fly twenty-five missions. We would certainly not have enough Tornadoes to fly them in.

Towards the end of the war all our bombing missions were exclusively laser-guided. Furthermore, the weather came to play a much more important role in our day-to-day operations. The days, weeks and months of brilliant sunshine and clear, blue skies gave way to a good deal of cloud cover. But it wasn't just cloud cover – we were flying through the smoke and foul fumes of the burning oilfields of Kuwait. This conflagration was blanketing vast areas of Iraq, often shrouding viable targets.

On Monday, 25 February we were again tasked to deliver our laser-guided bombs on the dreaded airfield where, a week before, we had seen two comrades shot down. The target was still a tough nut to crack and our crews had been trying for weeks to completely immobilize enemy forces. The weather was awful and formations were regularly coming back to base with their full weapons load still on board.

But our leaders decided we had to go. The blindingly obvious fact is that laser-guided bombing requires good visibility. If the target is obscured by cloud or smoke, it will disperse the laser energy, so that there is insufficient to guide the bombs. An unguided laser bomb can go anywhere. So I took very little interest in the early planning of our sorties but I always took a great interest in the weather.

Nearly twenty-four hours before we were due to engage the target, I went along to the weather office. It was a little hut in a corner of the airfield, manned by three rather nervous civilian meteorologists. They did a marvellous job. Their hastily assembled kit of state-of-the-art technology gave a pretty good picture and their forecasts were invariably accurate. I got from them the shortest weather brief of the war. One of the guys simply said, 'No chance.' The target would be totally obscured by cloud.

At that early stage I then requested for our weapons load to be changed from laser-guided to iron bombs, so we could use our radar to reach the target. Of course, they would not have the same pinpoint accuracy but at least we would be able to achieve something. My request was denied, perhaps in the hope of a change in the weather.

With twelve hours to go and our detailed planning complete, the weather had not changed. Again, my further request for a change in our weapons was refused.

With no time left, we were in the cockpit with our engines running. The only thing left was to lower the canopy and taxi to war again. One of the Buccaneer crew, navigator Dickie Aitken, who had become a good friend, walked by my jet. He had just returned from the same target and had been forced to overfly the airfield only two hours before. He looked up at me and shook his head from side to side. I could see a look of despair in his face that confirmed the futility of the mission he had just flown. He drew one hand across his throat as he gave me a thumbs down.

Without exchanging one word, because of the jet noise, and because I was plugged into the aircraft intercom, Dickie had told me we did not have a snowflake's chance in hell of reaching that target.

I called up on the radio to our ops desk. I wanted to explain we had just had a recent eyeball report of the weather in the target area. The weather was crap. Could we shut down?

We were told to go to the target, so we went and we overflew the target. It was totally hidden by cloud, so we returned to our base, having spent four hours in the air for no reason.

What's more, two other missions had flown ahead of mine that afternoon. That day, not one Tornado from Bahrain dropped one bomb. Around twenty aircraft with around forty aircrews had been exposed to the dangers of war for no reason. We all knew the weather was bad. We had made reasonable requests for weapons changes and they had been denied.

At the end of the war I asked a very senior officer why we had been sent that day, and on several other missions, knowing we would be bringing our bombs home. He waffled on, giving some political explanation that I still don't understand.

The target area was obscured by cloud and the route in was also in dense cloud. That also meant we had to refuel under the same tricky conditions and we had to fly in close formation through this weather over enemy airspace. It was crazy.

With that marvellous gift of hindsight, it is easy to say, 'Didn't we do well?' Yes, we did do bloody well. We lost miraculously few aircraft and miraculously few ground troops. Here we are, patting ourselves on the back. Yet I wonder if the same British Government would still be in power if the Iraqis had put up more of a fight and if, rather than tens of casualties, we had lost thousands.

Ironically, after that utterly futile mission, the frustration was spread right across the Air Force. Sure enough, our new orders for future missions were not to fly in bad weather and, sure enough, our next day's sortie was cancelled.

On 28 February, at 8 a.m. local time, President George Bush declared a ceasefire. My war was over.

At the time, we were busy preparing for our next mission. When the ceasefire came, everyone was cautious about dropping their guard. We had been fooled before, on 15 February, just a day after Rupert and Hicksey were shot down by two missiles.

The following day we were not scheduled to fly and I was on my way to visit our expat friends, John and Nuala Wright, who had made their lives in Bahrain.

They were full of the news that the war was

'over'. Hadn't I really heard? It had been reported on Bahraini Radio . . . Wonderful news. I was euphoric. I wanted to dance in the streets, to hug the first person I met. We had not just done our job well – we had been brilliant.

But I was not prepared for the terrible sadness and emptiness that suddenly clouded my thoughts. We had lost Rupert and Hicksey, for we all believed then they had both died. They had joined my team for one futile bombing mission the day before. It was now to be our last and it had cost them their lives. I could only think of the waste. Why did those boys have to die?

I wanted to be on my own. I had nothing to share with those people who wanted to dance in the streets as though they had just recovered from some terrible life-threatening illness. I crept out of my friends' dining-room, where they were toasting the peace, and climbed up the stairs to the roof terrace. I sat out there, in the bright sunshine, and cried my heart out. I didn't even know then that the amnesty offered by Saddam Hussein would prove false. I was very deeply shocked by the dejection and emptiness that I felt. It was a terrible sense of waste, all because of the acts of one madman.

I stayed up there for an hour, alone with my thoughts. Then I dried my eyes, took a shower and joined my friends for that drink. Less than a few hours later, we heard that the war would be going on. But I believe I discovered how I would feel when it was really over.

That night I took my boys and our two friends

171

to the Hash House Thai restaurant in town. I
excused myself from the rather subdued dinner
party at 9.30 p.m. and went to bed. I slept like a
baby for eleven hours.

It is not surprising that when the final ceasefire
came, no one dared believe it was really true. We
had all gone through that terrible stop-start two
weeks before. The latest news had travelled like
a bushfire through the base, but everyone waited.
We cautiously carried on with that day's tasks. The
whole of my formation was still hard at work,
planning as normal, but in our hearts I believe we
were all hoping and praying it would be over.

Around that base there were plenty of men with
weariness etched on their faces as they pored over
yet another detailed brief.

Everyone had worried for the ground troops. We
knew our job was to help save their lives, to minimize
casualties. But there was no doubt we had probably
gone on for just as long as we could.

When the official word came down, there was very
little celebrating: a few firm handshakes, the odd pat
on the back. There was no wild party that night.
The boys split up into twos and threes for a few
quiet beers.

It was a time to reflect. It was all over. There were
very few physical scars, but there would be many
mental scars that needed time to heal. Our lives had
been held on the pause button, and we now wanted
to get on with them. For me, seeing my family, Sheila
and the kids, became a priority.

You could see an immediate change in the boys

while we were still at our airbase during those dying hours of the war. There had been months of me issuing orders, instructions and detailed plans for one sortie after another without question. But now I had a revolt on my hands. I had great trouble organizing the boys for just a few last-minute photographs around our aircraft. It was now time to get on with our lives.

Very shortly after the end of the war a senior RAF officer stood in front of a crowd of well-wishers at a news conference. He was thoroughly enjoying all the backslapping as he proudly announced to the world that, with only a small percentage of the total aerial assets on the Allied side, the RAF had statistically flown twice as many bombing missions as anyone else. It struck me that he meant we had all flown those missions, often believing we would never come back alive, just to prove those bloody statistics.

Disraeli said, 'There are lies, damned lies and there are statistics.' Now I know that his words were true.

Even more Gulf War statistics have emerged, naturally all emphasizing the absolute success of the tactical planning. Statistically, well under one per cent of flying losses occurred on any sortie. Well, to put the record straight, I actually lost one quarter of my own formation on one such sortie – and that's twenty-five per cent.

If I or any of my comrades had been lost during battle, that would be 100 per cent of that aircrew gone, just as 100 per cent of me was lucky to come home alive.

I am sickened when I pick up military magazines advertising the supreme virtue of the JP233 bomb. Most of my comrades who were killed died on missions intended to deliver this horrendous weapon. During the very early stages of its development, the Americans actually pulled out of its production. They had recognized it was a suicidal weapon to deliver.

I am deeply disillusioned by the way in which the Royal Air Force has chosen to take a political attitude to the Gulf War. They are happy to hide behind statistics on losses: aircraft losses, aircrew losses.

It is too painful to the widows of many of these tragic men for me to name them, but more aircrews were actually killed during those frantic months of preparation than during the war. They died before hostilities began, yet their names have not been added to any Gulf War roll of honour. Their losses have not been added to the statistics, because they would make the figures look wrong.

After the final ceasefire, I don't believe the army had more than 100 hours of sweeping up to perform. Yet as soon as we had fulfilled our tasks, we were then messed around from backside to breakfast. Within hours of the ceasefire, we were promised we could go home within four days. Then hours later we were told it could be weeks, possibly a month. A day later it had turned into a three-month stay.

We had fought a war, won a war, lost comrades for that war. It was just a tea break and then back on your heads, boys. I was desperately angry at how we were treated. One idiot decreed that we should be ordered back to routine training missions and, sure enough, on 16 March I led a four-ship. We flew stupidly, with little regard for our safety. We had come so far and now a pointless official decision had left us disconsolate and taking mindless, crazy risks with our lives. It was obvious that the end of the war had come as a complete surprise to our superiors. There were no real plans, no organization to ensure that aircrews were delivered home to their loved ones as quickly and as painlessly as it could clearly have been done.

There were other aircrews, back in our bases in Germany and in the UK, who were clamouring to get out to the Gulf and climb into our cockpits. They had already been out to the Gulf. These crews had trained right up until the outbreak of war. They envied us, but we envied them too.

In one of the many relaxed and happy telephone conversations with our families, they told us how the church bells were pealing around our home bases at the news of the ceasefire. Our loved ones shared in our own huge sense of relief. They could now enjoy a night of peaceful sleep after weeks of anguish. But I could never offer a simple answer to the question that was constantly on the lips of my two children: 'When are you coming home, Daddy?'

In the weeks before, we had been fêted as warriors and honoured as brave men of war. Now we were no more than children.

I remember chatting to Colin Ayton just a few days after the ceasefire. I hadn't seen Chris Lunt around and so I asked Colin where his crewman had gone. Colin didn't know what had happened to his pal. But it transpired that he had been dispatched on an 'important' assignment, and had been taken away. I now know that he was involved in helping to identify the returned bodies of our dead comrades and in assisting with the rehabilitation of the men who had been held as POWs.

Our frustration grew as orders came down from our base commander not to discuss the names of any men who had been released by the Iraqis; or even to talk about the ones who had sadly not survived the war.

To my great joy, my old wingman John Peters telephoned me one day from RAF Akrotiri in Cyprus, where he had been taken after his release from Iraq. He had a shopping list of gifts he had always planned to take home for his wife, Helen, and their two small children before his untimely departure from Bahrain.

He wanted a rosewood table, a smart camera and a few trinkets for his wife and children. I was delighted to help my old pal out of a fix and buy them on his behalf. He was delighted to be alive, and his voice was full of hope and joy. Yet I had been forbidden to reveal to my own wife, Sheila, that John had been freed from that Iraqi hell-hole and that he had called me to speak of his release.

The world had watched on TV the moment that our other John, John Nichol, and the pilot Rupert Clark climbed down the steps of an aeroplane at Dahran to freedom. Rupert *was* alive, and now he was free.

But in our phone calls home we had to pretend to our loved ones that we knew nothing about their release. From warriors to children in one fell swoop, and all it took was a ceasefire. I was once a leader of seven men, but now I was an unwanted number among many. We were no longer the liberating forces. We were a problem to the military machine; to those suppliers, mobility men, who must now move thousands of us back to our bases in Germany and the UK.

Members of my own team vanished overnight without a word. They had been sent off on an important task without even the chance to say a brief farewell to the comrades they had fought so bravely alongside.

Our wingmen, Bob Brownlow and Jack Calder, were lucky to be among the early ones to return home to their base. They had hurriedly flown out to us after the loss of the two Johns and all they had with them was the small amount of baggage they could load on board in some tiny compartment of their Tornado. Bob only had one pair of shoes with him, but both men lived alongside the rest of us without complaint for those months.

It was only right that they should be sent home ahead and so they flew a Tornado out to Tabuk then joined a trail of aircraft returning from Tabuk. They would be home two weeks before the rest of us.

Just before they departed, Bob shook me by the hand and I thanked him for all his help. I told him that I hoped to see him in the future and meet the wife and family he loved so dearly. Then I suggested that perhaps he would like me to convey his good wishes to our squadron commander at Muharraq. Bob said perhaps I might also say hello to the boss on his behalf, because, throughout the entire war, he had not even met him.

I have subsequently learned many things about my role in the war. I have learned, both officially and unofficially, that our squadron boss offered up a good deal of criticism about my style of leadership. In his opinion, my formation had been one of the most difficult to administer and to task. I had given the ops staff and the base organizers a good deal of hassle as we prepared for each mission. Well, I believe that was one of my prime tasks as a leader. I was certainly going to ride their backs just as hard as I could to get the best possible support for my boys. Because we were going to do the best possible job and I wanted everyone, right there, behind us.

If any Ministry of Defence statistician would care to look at what my team achieved, I think the results will appear admirable. We flew the first daylight ultra-low-level mission, we flew the first night medium-level mission and we flew the first laser-guided bombing mission. We also flew the most complex mission of the whole war, when we were tasked against two airfields in one sortie. Never once, on any tasked mission, did I personally fail to get through to the target. My team produced, statistically or otherwise, among the finest results of the war.

# 6

# Loyalty

The Royal Air Force pays a particularly high regard to loyalty. This loyalty it requires of its airmen and of its officers, both to the ideals of the service and to the needs of the service. In an officer or an airman's confidential report, the commander is required to assess, on a scale of one to nine, the degree of loyalty displayed by that individual.

I have always believed that in order to command loyalty, it is necessary to show the same loyalty in return. In much the same way, a faithful hound will display loyalty to its master, but it expects, in return, to be fed, to be offered some reward and, on occasion, to be shown some affection.

As a young junior officer on my first helicopter squadron, I often spent time on a commanding officer's carpet after coming fairly close to the limits. After an episode of some tomfoolery or other I would be there to receive admonishment, along with a group of my closest friends and colleagues who had got into trouble with me. To take one example, at first we had only intended to pour a bucketful of water into the station commander's car. But inevitably we got

179

carried away and ended up putting a hosepipe through the window and filling the car with water.

Likewise, we had planned to put a little sand into the double bed of the newly married young officer and his wife while they were away on honeymoon. But one thing led to another and when they returned they were horrified to discover the entire ground floor of their new quarters had been bricked up: front door, windows and all. They spent a good few hours with a hammer and chisel before the groom could even carry his now furious young bride over the threshold of their first home together.

My Flight Commander had tried all ways of getting me to see sense. Perhaps he did have an effect because I had certainly always admired him. But, more often than not, I continued enjoying life to the absolute full while doing my job to the best of my ability. After one fairly protracted spell of high jinx, which ended – I can't remember – either after I had blown up an entire flower-bed on a German airbase, or dents had been discovered in a Land Rover in which I was teaching my dog to drive, the Squadron Commander decided there was little that could be done but to make an example of me to other junior officers.

The general consensus was that this time I had gone too far and would probably be out of the squadron within a matter of weeks. I tried desperately to maintain as low a profile as possible as I anxiously waited for my commanding officer's decision. After a few weeks of nervous anticipation, I was summoned into my Flight Commander's office. He was a career man, very dapper, and he has since gone a long way in the RAF. I still greatly admire him for his handling of one very badly behaved and out of control young officer.

'Well, Pablo,' he began, 'I expect you already know what is in store for you. I have spoken to the Squadron Commander, who is certain that he wants to see you off his squadron. I have told him that if you go, then I shall go as well. I think he has perhaps decided that I am much too good a Flight Commander to lose, so it looks like you will be staying as well.

'You are going to stay and you will remain on my flight. But don't worry, for the next year or so I am going to personally make your life hell. Just be grateful for it.'

Grateful! I was over the moon.

I had been an irritating thorn in the side of my Flight Commander. I had caused more mayhem socially than any other person since he arrived on the station a few months after me. Professionally, I had done a very good job. But that wasn't everything, and whenever there was trouble after some high jinks I would be hauled in. And he well knew that after I had been admonished for my behaviour by the Squadron Commander, he would be next in line for a bollocking for failing to keep me in line.

But when it came to the crunch and higher authorities had all but decided that he had failed in his job to make me toe the line, he took my side. He put himself on the line as a display of loyalty to me. Perhaps in those early days, it was a loyalty I did not really deserve. After all, I had failed to support his command by causing so much mayhem on the base.

He did go on to make my life hell and I was always in line for extra duties, but I never let him down again.

On my first Tornado squadron, almost six years ago, one of the Squadron Commanders there was a tyrant. He always demanded 110 per cent of his men. Whatever we did never seemed good enough and he would work himself all the hours God sent, to prove how it should be done. He certainly practised what he preached, but many times he brought us very close to breaking point.

A young officer who, I suppose, many of us regarded as a ne'er-do-well, had been caught drink-driving. Initial rumours suggested that not only would he suffer an astonishingly expensive fine and be banned from driving for a year, but he would also find himself removed from the squadron. Perhaps he would end up out of a job.

To be honest, I didn't like this chap too much. No one appeared to be rooting for him until it became evident that the only person he had on his side was the Squadron Commander. This man, whom we all regarded as something of a hard taskmaster, was a thirty-eight-year-old Wing Commander. He was destined for the top and today he is not far from that position. He had nothing to lose by not showing his loyalty to this junior officer who had displayed a flagrant disregard for the regulations and for common sense.

But, whether or not he saw some spark in this young man, he was the only one who stood by him. Push almost came to shove because the commanders in their ivory tower at RAF Headquarters Germany really wanted an example made of the younger man. But the Squadron Commander simply refused to budge. He would not allow the demise of a young officer who belonged to him and was in his charge. I think that junior officer learned a lot about loyalty and its two faces: upwards and downwards. He never let his Squadron Commander down again and went on to become a very successful and well-respected fast-jet pilot in the RAF.

In my full and varied military career, I have been blessed with good and bad bosses, strong and weak bosses, bosses who have made it very easy for me to show them loyalty and those who have made it hard for me to even offer them my loyalty.

Throughout that time, I have regarded my devotion to the Royal Air Force as almost unswerving. There were several occasions during the year or so before the Gulf War had ever been considered, when the loyalty I had shown that service was repaid in full.

I have had my fair share of domestic troubles. But when I called for help to sort out those family problems it was freely given by my bosses. There was no difficulty over time off to try to put my family first for a change. And there was never a whiff of recriminations because, for a short time, I had been unable to put a 100 per cent effort into my job.

However, on one or two occasions the alarm bells have rung: perhaps when I was being asked to do much more than I could hope to see in return. The summer of 1988 was an idyllic time for me. I had recently been promoted into a new job on a new squadron. But I was still living in the same officer's home that Sheila and I had shared since we first moved out to Germany four years before.

It was a pleasant house in a semi-detached quarter in a nice little village in Germany, close to the border with Holland. Then it looked as though everything was really going our way. The commitments of one of our satellite stations had just been reduced and a senior officer had moved away, so that his luxury quarters became vacant. He had thoroughly enjoyed this large, detached house with a huge, private garden. When we were offered that house, we jumped at the chance.

There would be some expense because we were expected to pay our own removal costs. We would have to clean our old home from top to bottom before marching out and then we were expected to clean up the new place. But we were delighted with the arrangements. Our children would have an extra-large bedroom each. We would also have a spare guest room and Sheila would now have her own dressing room. We had a huge garage adjoining the house where I could keep the old Jensen that I had been lovingly restoring for the past five years.

Then, within days of moving into our plush new quarters, it seemed that the service had changed its plans. A more senior officer now required the accommodation we had just taken over. We were instructed to vacate the property at once. I wrote endless letters asking for some leeway over this. I discovered that the officer who was due to take over our new home would be living there with just his wife.

Their children had long since grown up and moved away. Surely they would have been better off in our old home. It was smaller to take care of and the rent was considerably cheaper.

Each letter I wrote was politely and diplomatically answered but no one was going to budge. Within weeks our little dream turned into a terrible nightmare. We moved house twice and ended up back where we started, but now we were out of pocket too.

We were left with a terrible sense of disappointment about the way we had been treated by the service I served and my family were obliged to respect. But a commanding officer somewhere had decided the senior officer should rightfully demand our new home. It was all rearranged so very neatly as the Wing Commanders on the station hid behind their leather-bound volumes of the Queen's Regulations. It was all so very unfair.

In May of 1990, only months before we were to be involved in the hellish preparations for the Gulf War, my XV Squadron enjoyed an idyllic weekend in the company of many old boys as we celebrated our seventy-fifth anniversary. The occasion for me had been extra special because I had been the project officer in charge of organizing the weekend events. To steal a phrase that made history only eight months later in entirely different circumstances, the whole event 'ran on rails'. I had sweated blood during the months and weeks in the build-up to this prestigious celebration. It was a success, thanks to the many junior officers who had made up my committee and had worked so hard to ensure everything ran smoothly.

As the weekend drew closer I realized there would be one of two results. If, for whatever reason, the whole event proved to be a failure, the blame would rest squarely on my shoulders. If, as it was, a success, then the glory would more than likely be taken by an officer senior to me. I always knew what the letters OBE stood for. They mean Other Buggers' Efforts. I felt rewarded enough by the weekend itself, by seeing the joy in some of those old boys' faces, men who had once flown Blenheims and Stirling Bombers way back in the Second World War. But I also felt damned frustrated for some of the younger men on my team. They had worked very hard and should have been recognized for it, at least with some small accolade in their annual confidential report. That document is guaranteed to have a dramatic effect on an officer's progress through the ranks.

It should never matter that a reporting officer either likes or dislikes the individual concerned, who may be something of a rough diamond or even a bit of a social outcast. What really did matter in this case was that those boys had proved their organizational skills and their dedication to a task.

History repeated itself during the early months of 1991. There were then, and there still are, very many untapped resources in the RAF. Young men went to war and performed with dedication and bravery. Many surprised me, and they must have also surprised our commanders. But when they came home from war they were treated no differently from the youngsters who had fought their war from an office desk at our home bases.

Some had played no real part in the war at all. It is hard to know what the RAF really does expect of its junior officers. The vast majority of the aircrew involved in the Gulf conflict were junior officers, flight lieutenants and even flying officers. Most of them were in their early to mid-twenties. Yet the vast majority of honours and awards medals were handed out to senior officers, squadron leaders and even more senior ranks.

It's true to say that before the war, with one or two unhappy exceptions, the Air Force showed me the loyalty that I offered in return. Even when we were working desperately hard during the build-up to war, many of my own comrades happily put in more hours so that I could take time off in October and November 1990 to take, and pass, examinations for my civilian flying licence.

But shortly after the war it seemed that the Air Force now demanded some penance before it would show me any loyalty at all.

The Gulf War irrevocably changed many of our lives. The guys who were kept back at home gave up many hours at night to help the war effort and support the flying crews. But they had not actually fought in the war and now, in March, we were back on their territory.

We were all men changed by our experience of war. But if we were to succeed in today's modern Air Force, we must simply change back again. The quickest way of doing that would have been for us all to conveniently vanish back into the woodwork. But I don't believe that many of us could.

I am an easy person to focus upon. I am a flamboyant character; I wear an aviator's handlebar moustache. The reporters who followed us through the war quickly picked me out for their television and newspaper coverage. I honestly didn't mind their attention; in fact I probably enjoyed much of it. I have always believed in telling the truth about how I felt and about what was happening to me. I have nothing to fear from the truth.

What I do know for a fact is that the squadron boss strongly disapproved of the way in which I dealt with the media's attention and the way in which I displayed many of my emotions. Yes, I was one of those brave warriors who cried in front of the cameras at the loss of two of my comrades in battle. Was that such a terrible thing to do?

Just before I left the squadron he told me that he had described my attitude as, at best, naïve. During the Gulf War he never personally told me how he felt about me but he did everything in his power to make sure those opinions were passed on to me through others. I believe that my boss showed, in many ways, the most tremendous naïvety that I have ever witnessed from a senior officer. During his time at Muharraq, his position was that of Tornado detachment commander in charge of all squadrons based there.

There were aircrews from IX Squadron also based in Germany, and 27 and 617 Squadrons from the UK. Yet it occurred to me and to many of my comrades that our boss never stopped being OC for just XV Squadron. It just seemed that if we hadn't been on that same XV Squadron, then we would not have been worthy of his consideration.

For the record, perhaps it is worth pointing out that, of all the aircrew based at Muharraq, the majority were not on XV Squadron. Only one honour of a Mention in Despatches went to an aircrew that was not part of XV Squadron.

My view that Muharraq appeared to be staffed by XV Squadron and then the rest, was shared by a number of the other guys. One four-ship leader who was leaving the Gulf a few weeks before me bade me farewell. He told me that he would also have liked to remind my squadron commander that his squadron had also been there fighting alongside XV.

After I finally came home from the war on 23 March 1991 I quickly realized that my loyalty to the service I had so loved was not so much in question as the loyalty I believed it owed me. Many of my comrades who had endured fear and misery in Iraqi jails, and others who had bravely fought and carried out one bombing mission after another, were expected to slide back into obscurity almost as soon as the ceasefire was declared. They appeared to have become something of an embarrassment to the service they had so loyally served during the war.

How many times have I heard from young officers that it is not the RAF's way to expect any individual or even collective recognition when we were only doing our jobs. The men who fought alongside me and were killed were only doing their jobs too. So were those aircrew who were shot down, captured and tortured by the enemy.

We all knew we were out there to do the job we had all trained for. But no one ever expected that we would be called upon to fight a war. One very senior officer once told me that any man who signed up for the RAF or any other service, hoping he would be called upon to go and fight, was not the right man for the services.

After the ceasefire it was felt by many crews that they were something of a problem for the RAF. This was partly because the public, who had given us so much support, now wanted to see some display of respect and gratitude. The war refused to lie down.

I still believe that the brave young men who always wanted to be RAF pilots and briefly enjoyed acclaim during the Gulf War, will sink into obscurity. Because it is certain the RAF no longer wants to present them as heroes.

When I left the RAF in November 1991, it was after eighteen wonderful years. But those final months were the unhappiest of my entire career. I know I was not alone with those feelings.

The repatriation of all the troops from the Gulf, including the POWs, was a mixture of chaos and pandemonium. Every one of them, as he was released from captivity and handed over to the Red Crescent, was then linked up with a mentor as soon he was finally handed back to our own forces.

This companion, a man from his own squadron, was there to help him through those first, difficult days of liberation. Wherever possible, this person would be an old and trusted friend. Of course, three of the POWs, John Peters, John Nichol and Rupert Clark, were all men from my own squadron. This meant that three other men from the squadron who had flown in the war would be seconded to act as their mentors.

These men were quickly and secretly removed from our company in the Gulf. For days we often had no idea where they had gone or what they were doing. After months of sharing our lives with them we now had no right to know where they were going.

The POWs were all brought home to waving banners, bands playing and VIP receptions on the tarmac. John Peters was the first to return to our base at Laarbruch. He arrived at nightfall to the waiting press, RAF VIPs, and his wife, Helen, and their two small children tucked away around the corner waiting for a private reunion.

All the prisoners deserved every moment of glory at their triumphant homecoming from the terror and torture they had so bravely endured. The world wanted to see them and the RAF put them on a rostrum for all the world to see. But the companions who had gently shepherded them through those early days in transit from the Middle East to RAF Akrotiri in Cyprus and then home were no longer required. They had acted as a sponge for the men who had endured so much in captivity. These guys had also fought in the war and had then been summoned to leave at a moment's notice, without a chance to pack up their own few belongings.

As the cameras clicked to capture the wonderful

moment of freedom for the POWs, who were being fêted as heroes, their comforters were whisked away. They were curtly informed that their services were no longer needed, and left to find their own way home to their families.

Many of these companions had been selected because they had shown a spare capacity to soak up some of the emotion that the POWs so desperately needed to share. But after the shock of such an unhappy homecoming, they too experienced a trauma that many will not talk about even now. They didn't want or even expect to be placed on a rostrum alongside the former POWs. But some had not even been given the chance to inform their own families that they too were coming home from war.

Surely there was a place for them too, as the nation showed its heartfelt thanks for the safe return of brave young men like John Peters. Perhaps they should have got a thank you from their RAF seniors in recognition of the countless missions they had flown, the terrors they too had endured before putting their emotions aside to assist those considered more needy.

Psychologists and psychiatrists have long known about the traumas that many men face as they return home from war. Undoubtedly there will always be a handful of people who escape the attention they need in the frenzied mish-mash known as the recovery home.

I was one of the lucky ones, for I came home to a wonderful champagne reception of waiting family and friends along with most of my squadron comrades. There was a reception on 23 March, organized by the men who had stayed behind at our base. I shall never forget that day and I am sure many of my fellow men who served in the conflict feel the same way. It was right that every effort should have been made to ensure that as few people as possible fell through the net. But in the case of the guys who brought home the POWs, they didn't exactly fall through the net – they were pushed.

One of my very dearest friends was a companion to one of the POWs. I don't think his name is really important for this story. But I am sure that even now he still feels deep disappointment and resentment towards the service that so wilfully ignored his own homecoming. When the welcome mat was put out, it was left there just long enough for our first POW, John Peters, to step on it before it was pulled away again.

My friend was determined that such ignominy would not befall other comrades who would soon be returning with our comrades Rupert Clark and John Nicol. He set up his own little reception committee of wives and friends for the other men who would be coming home from the war alongside them. The RAF officials and waiting press were only interested in seeing the freed prisoners; in learning what had befallen them and how they had been treated.

The rest had just fought a war, day in day out, and come home again. They were not important. But my pal made sure there was champagne on ice and banners flying as they came down the steps of the RAF VC10. From the net that he had been earlier pushed through, he had made a safety net underneath.

I slept for almost the entire journey from Muharraq to our eventual landing at RAF Laarbruch. I don't know if it was a sleep that would help prepare me for the future, but I was certainly nervous about what lay ahead of me in life. After such a long time to reflect, I now realize that I probably needed help at that time to readjust to peace. I wasn't alone in that need. I'm not sure if I was suffering from fatigue, confusion or perhaps even sheer apathy. But I could never find the energy or the confidence to go out and seek help or guidance from the organization I had served. I had stepped straight down from an aeroplane to my family and a champagne reception. Then I simply signed a couple of forms before I went off on five weeks' leave.

Ringing in my ears had been the reassurance that any request for help, either mental or physical, would always be provided. I don't know if that was even true. Maybe it was meant in spirit, but in practice I'm not sure that any of us were helped through some difficult days after the war was over.

Certainly, one of the POWs was assured by medical staff, months after he was released, that the back injury he had sustained from ejection had now healed. No one seemed to suspect that his pain may have arisen from the anguish he still suffered as a result of his experiences. But I saw the agony on that man's face; the pain he believed came from a back injury that the RAF had told him he did not have.

For many of us, that month or so after coming home was like very slowly coming round from a general anaesthetic. There wasn't just a physical numbness, but a mental numbness too. I believe there should have been some provision made to help us all recover in our own time, or at least the many who honestly admitted they needed help.

In November 1991 I saw a television programme about the release and rehabilitation of the Beirut hostage Jackie Mann. The Royal Air Force had stepped in to offer its excellent facilities at RAF Lyneham in Wiltshire, to assist in his gentle rehabilitation over a number of days. He wasn't casually offered help; it was assumed that that fine old man, who had loyally and bravely served his country years before, would need and be given the best help that was available to bring him steadily back into the world. The RAF pulled out all the stops for Jackie Mann, as they did for John McCarthy before and then finally for the Archbishop of Canterbury's special envoy Terry Waite. They were all fine men, who well deserved the attention and consideration they received.

But for the boys returning from the Gulf, there was nowhere near enough done to assist in their rehabilitation. Of course, we had only gone out and done our jobs because that is what we had been trained for. There had been months of hard preparation for war. But we had received no training, help or guidance on what to expect once that war was over. Whether we had achieved victory or not, the RAF back in Germany wanted nothing more than to get us back to our bases and forget it ever really happened.

I began to feel that I was an incredible burden to the system and that in itself made me reluctant to ask for counselling, as though that would make me an even bigger burden. I was dejected, tired and lonely. The only people I could share my experiences with were the men I had fought alongside. I didn't want to be considered important or highly valued like some prize peacock. No, I desperately wanted to feel that I still belonged and was wanted by the system I had left behind months before. But I never really felt that I belonged again.

The POWs did appear to be properly and care-fully handled when they first returned home. They received the finest medical attention, both physical and psychological. They were offered the use of VIP chalets and country houses around Berlin. They were fostered, nurtured and brought back into the fold and made to feel important by the world at large.

However, at a very early stage, the Air Force tried to use them like puppets. At one point they were all press-ganged into personally signing 1000 limited-edition prints of a watercolour by the artist Eric Day, depicting a few Tornadoes flying over the desert. Of course, with the added attraction of the signatures of a handful of former POWs, the prints were worth a good deal of money. They were sold to raise cash for the RAF Benevolent Fund. The objectives were honourable enough; the funds were being raised for a worthy cause. But when I spoke to one of those boys at length, he told me how angry and bitter he now felt at the way he had been used. It was not very different from the champion racehorse Red Rum opening countless supermarkets.

He told me that he had not been asked to kindly provide his signature in aid of a worthy cause. He was simply told his signature was required. He didn't discover what it was all about until one day when he was in the bank at our base. There he noticed a poster publicizing the sale of the prints, which would be on special offer to members of the armed forces. It was news to him.

Each of the POWs had his own views on how he wanted to tell the clamouring world his story – or not, in some cases. One or two wanted to talk to the papers. Other men had already firmly decided that whatever terrible torture they had endured was a very private part of their lives and would stay firmly in the past.

Any wife who wanted to sell a story, whether as a book or as an interview with a national newspaper, had every right to do so. The nonsense talked about the necessity for restrictions on former POWs for 'security' reasons was no more than a smokescreen.

The RAF eventually decided that it would arrange a press conference at which three POWs would tell the story of their ordeal in an Iraqi jail. All this came after they had been denied a perfectly reasonable right to arrange their own, private transactions with publishers or newspaper editors.

The arrangements suited some of the guys, but angered others, who felt they were about to be paraded on stage like so many puppets and tried to refuse to take part. They made little secret of their frustrations and, eventually, in a bid to put a stop to this circus, their story was leaked to the newspapers. Of course, as soon as the story broke, the Ministry of Defence mandarins appeared both surprised and hurt that anyone could suggest these men were being forced to do something against their will.

The press conference was hastily abandoned by the MoD until they could come up with some other plan. Finally, POWs Robbie Stewart and Dave Waddington were persuaded to give an account of their captivity for a book called *Thunder and Lightning*, about the RAF's role in the Gulf War. It had been entirely orchestrated and controlled by the MoD in London.

It will come as no surprise that neither of those boys received any recognition for revealing what must have been a very painful story. The whole episode created a very bad odour among us all.

I was amazed at how little John Peters, John Nichol and Rupert Clark seemed to have changed as a result of their terrible ordeal. The two Johns were still every bit as bright and bubbly. Rupert was the quiet type, but oozing with self-confidence. Those boys were the same as I ever remembered them and they did their best to act as normally as possible after they came home.

It's not surprising that they wanted to hear our war stories too; especially the two Johns, who had sadly missed so much of the action. They both tried very hard to cast aside the international media attention that was being thrust upon them. They were perhaps a little embarrassed at all the interest they had generated by being paraded on TV by their Iraqi captors.

John Peters could not believe that he was now in public demand. The two Johns' appearance at the RAF Mildenhall Air Show was enough to raise more than £20,000 for the RAF Benevolent Fund from autograph signings. The public simply loved them. It wasn't their fault, but they had, unwittingly, become a little bit of public property.

The boys wanted desperately to be back, as part of the team. But they appeared on *Wogan* as national heroes and they were reported almost daily in the newspapers. They were photographed at the Gulf Parade in the City of London and they were pictured flying again together for the first time after they had been shot down.

Sadly, they also began to be resented by some of the men who had not been captured but had gone on to fly endless bombing missions. There were the odd sarcastic comments about the fact that no one seemed interested in any of the other guys. 'You had to miss the target and get yourself shot down to be noticed', was one particularly unkind comment that was bandied around about them.

It was very unfair. Maybe they didn't really deserve all this public attention. But all the POWs I met acted with absolute propriety. They didn't see themselves as national heroes. But they should never have seen themselves as anything less of a hero than any one of us who flew to war. Anyone who resents their little moment of glory after months in captivity should ask himself: who in God's name would have swapped places with them during the war?

One particularly outrageous edict that came down to us during the war was the announcement that the flying pay of officers who had been shot down and captured would be withdrawn. Flying pay is a separate addition to the salaries of aircrew and it is payable whenever crew are available to fly. That does not mean we have to be on a flying tour to receive this bonus. We simply had to be available.

But someone flying a desk was more interested in the letter of the law. Consequently, if some of the men were now languishing in Iraqi jails, they were no longer available to fly and therefore did not qualify for flying pay.

It wasn't just the announcement that this pay would be withdrawn that caused such indignation. It was the way in which the wives of these men were told. Understandably, many already found it hard to cope with the fact that their men were missing in action. So imagine how they reacted to the contents of a brown HMSO letter landing on the doormat, telling them they should expect less in their husband's next salary cheque. The flying pay was now to be withdrawn because their husbands were not available to fly.

This ridiculous and astonishingly insensitive proposal, did not just cause outrage among the wives at home. When the news reached the front line, all the aircrews were angry. It is hardly surprising that the edict was very quickly repealed and hushed up to avoid a public outcry. I sincerely hope that the fool in the pay and allowances section who first issued this ruling had his knuckles very firmly rapped.

Many of us had taken out personal insurances before the war. We wanted to know that our families would be comfortably taken care of if we never came home. In addition to our own personal provisions, it was very reassuring to hear that the Gulf Fund was reaching incredible levels as cash poured in from a caring public.

At least the families of those brave boys who lost their lives in the war would receive financial support to help them over the coming years. I believe that none of the widows of aircrew who, like me, had sensibly taken out private insurance, received one penny from the Gulf Fund. They received nothing more than their husband's war pension and monies to which they were legitimately entitled. None of the funds sent in by generous people from all over Britain and the rest of the world ever found its way to the widows of some of these men. These women and their small children will hopefully live in some material comfort – thanks to the private insurance arranged by their husbands. But the Gulf Fund was set up for them too.

Many of those tragic families were forced to endure days of silence until the MoD officially published the details of those who were known to have died. Our wives told us how they had all known that a husband had been identified as missing in action after the Station Commander visited a nearby home.

But until it had been officially announced from Whitehall, no one could offer to comfort a wife or child, or even talk about a dear friend or close neighbour who had been lost. All the worried wives and the men who remained at our base found the atmosphere that this created almost intolerable. It was as if the tension and anguish over the ones who were fighting on the front line was not enough for them to bear. They must also be the victims of a hidebound bureaucracy. Wives would often simply disappear from their jobs on the base and a child would be taken out of school.

I was delighted when I read the Gulf honours list, especially to see that I was not among the honoured few. I would not shy away from honour or recognition. Like most of the boys who had actually managed to save their bacon and get home, I think some tribute to our deeds would have been appreciated. Yes, I would have appreciated a medal; I think I deserved one. I had led the first of a number of bombing missions using new techniques. I had also taken many risks to ensure that I got through to the target to achieve success on a mission.

Nevertheless, the honours list came as no surprise to me. I think I could have written that list of names before the first shot was fired. I've always regarded decorations such as the Distinguished Service Order and the Distinguished Flying Cross with tremendous respect and reverence; not just the medals but also the people who wear them. But what I saw of the Gulf honours list has tarnished my view of those medals for ever.

There were so many brave young men out there in the Gulf, and it is true that some missions were far more challenging than others. But, at the end of the war, it seemed that it no longer mattered how brave people had been or how challenging the missions that they had flown. All that counted was how well their individual achievements had been written up by their seniors.

Of course there were only so many medals available, but it still didn't matter how brave people had been. It just mattered that the medals were seen to be fairly dispersed throughout the units. But even that attempt failed. Very few navigators received Gulf medals. It was mostly senior officers who were rewarded for their bravery and other squadrons were almost totally ignored for their war effort. The Gulf honours list caused a good deal of discontent among the squadrons, for very obvious reasons. Many of my comrades well deserved individual recognition. But not all of them.

I am sure the Gulf honours were also used as a damn good way of getting back at certain individuals. None of this affects me now, because I have left the RAF. But it will certainly affect the careers of one or two Wing Commanders who fought and were given no recognition for their sterling work. Their careers have certainly been slowed down by whoever it was who wrote up those war reports and failed to maintain objectivity in recognizing individual bravery. Instead, they seized the opportunity to advance the careers of individuals they wanted to see get on in the RAF.

I could easily be accused of sour grapes. But it wouldn't be true. It came to me as no surprise that I did not receive an individual medal for the part I played in the Gulf War. It was patently obvious that I would not be recommended for an award. Not because I failed to do my duty or did not show bravery – even now I do not know if I was brave or not – but I was not singled out for honour because I have rarely seen eye to eye with the senior officer who wrote my report.

At the same time, all this makes me feel very sorry for my navigator, Gary Stapleton. Without doubt, he is one of the finest navigators on fast jets within the RAF. He was certainly one of the best who flew to war. Yet he received no recognition whatsoever for his ability, his dedication or his loyalty. I know that this was because he was flying in the same aeroplane as me.

After returning home towards the end of March 1991, and after a lengthy period of extended leave, we finally started flying again. On 2 May Gary and I flew our first sortie together again as a very enjoyable singleton. We flew off to the UK, dropped a few bombs on a range, refuelled from a waiting Victor tanker and we were back home in time for tea. It all seemed so normal and easy now that no one was firing at us any longer. It was a sortie that we both thoroughly enjoyed.

Eight days and four sorties later, on 10 May, I crashed an aircraft on the North German plain. From that day, the RAF showed me little or no loyalty and the loyalty I once had for the service diminished irrevocably.

It was a typical late-spring day for that part of the world. There was very little cloud cover but visibility was still restricted to about four miles. The plain itself was as flat as a pancake and we were back to our peacetime restrictions of not flying lower than 1000ft above the ground. The rules would certainly make any aspects of the sortie far simpler than anything any of us had known over the past six months.

My task, with Rob Woods as my navigator for the trip, was to fly as an aggressor aircraft against a formation of two other Tornadoes. They were attempting to get through to a simulated target. We all knew the precise route and timings. It was our job to simulate the threat from a Warsaw Pact fighter and attack the formation at the earliest opportunity.

Rob and I took off a few minutes before the formation pair behind us, and set up our first successful ambush. We got in among the formation and mauled them, giving our calls of simulated missile firings. We were already well within our parameters to shoot them down.

Our second attack was an equal success and we left them with their tails well between their legs. Now it was time to try to improve the situation for the cowed and beaten formation; to boost their morale a little and give them something to learn from. This was a training sortie after all. And so we positioned for a head-on attack against the formation. We would be heading north and they would be running south. The intercept would take place at around twenty miles east of Bremerhaven. It worked well, and I picked out one aircraft and then another on a reciprocal heading to me.

We had them right down the throat and all they had to do was pick us up visually, accelerate and keep running south. That way we would have been little or no threat to them. In the event, they didn't see us at all.

We were head on and I passed abeam the formation and started to turn in behind them.

At this very moment the whole world went absolutely haywire. My aircraft was turning hard, far harder than I wanted it to. As I relaxed the controls it seemed to want to turn even harder. I tried to take it out of its turn but it was determined to continue almost as though it wanted to vanish up its own jet pipe. The aircraft rolled and tucked. It had a mind of its own as it pitched towards the ground.

I realized then that we were about to crash. As I fought with the controls I screamed, 'Rob, Rob, Rob' over the intercom. I remember dipping into a small clearing and seeing trees ahead and all around me. Then there was a bang, a flash of flames in front of my eyes. I was being buffeted and thrown around.

I can recall counting the bangs: 'One, two, three, four.' I wondered which one was going to kill me. But then I felt a great jolt to my shoulders and the small of my back. All around me was quiet and I opened my eyes to see that I was facing the ground.

I wasn't suspended upright beneath my parachute harness, but almost on all fours. I thought: Oh crikey, I've survived whatever has gone wrong with my aircraft controls and now I am moments away from some horrific injury.

Something had also gone wrong with the retraction system on my harness to cause this ungainly posture beneath the billowing parachute. My fear was that whatever I was going to land on would do me no good at all. If I landed on soft, muddy ground, in this position I would probably suffocate. If I landed on hard ground I would almost certainly break my ankles, knees and face.

If I landed in water there was no way I could get at the parachute harness to release myself, and I would surely drown.

Someone upstairs in head office was obviously looking after me. I closed my eyes and hoped for the best. I landed in a tree and finished my descent rather ignominiously suspended about a foot from the ground without a scratch.

Rob had ejected us both from the stricken jet. He had certainly saved my life. The ejection and parachute descent to my final, merciful resting place had taken a total of a few seconds.

Rob landed in a field only a few yards from me. Although I couldn't see him, he approached from behind and called out to see if I was OK.

I was definitely OK. I was swearing blue murder. And for the first time in probably my entire RAF career, I said 'please' to a navigator. Rob insisted I say it nicely or he assured me he wouldn't release me from my unfortunate position in the tree.

Thankfully, Rob appeared to me to be completely unscathed after his experience. But I discovered I had a terrible chest pain every time I tried to stand up straight, so I remained crouching on the ground.

Rob scurried around like a mother hen, organizing fluorescent panels on the ground and inflating our dinghies. Their bright-orange canopies would attract the two Tornadoes that were now circling overhead looking for some sign that we had survived.

A German rescue helicopter arrived on the scene

in what seemed like no more than minutes and an American doctor attended to me. I told her my chest hurt. But after she tried to make me lie down straight it began to hurt like hell. Eventually she managed to push a needle into my arm and that was the last thing I remember for the next day and a half.

After a brief stay in a military hospital in Hamburg, we were both well enough to be transported to the Royal Air Force military hospital at Wegberg. The RAF supplied a Puma support helicopter and *en route* to the hospital we managed to persuade the crew to take us to the crash site. I was still heavily sedated but I can recall wandering, dazed, around the site wearing my light-blue pyjamas and my flying boots. I was shocked to see what was left of our jet. The wreckage was scattered over what seemed like acres of ground.

There was a deep black scar burned into the ground. It was only about 10ft wide, but it ran on for about 400 yards, ending up in a wood.

A large proportion of the trees had been burned away by some searing fire. The crash site was already under heavy guard by airmen, many of whom had been sent from my own base at Laarbruch. They were there to deter souvenir hunters in search of a piece of instrumentation or fuselage. There was little for them to scavenge but anything that had been left would be needed by the investigators who would attempt to discover the cause of the crash.

I had actually known some of the boys who were there while we were out in the Gulf. They shared my despair that I had managed to get through the conflict without a scratch yet within a few days of getting back to flying in Europe I had been forced to escape a stricken jet.

After we arrived at Wegberg with me strapped to a stretcher and Rob a sitting and walking patient, we discovered that Rob was far more badly injured than I had been. The x-rays revealed that my trouble was no more than heavy bruising and a couple of sprung ribs whereas Rob had fractured a couple of vertebrae and was confined to bed for three months.

Our families were waiting to see us, as was our commanding officer, and he seemed happy and relieved that we had both escaped alive. We would surely live to fly another day. Or so I thought.

Within hours we received the first of many visits from the board of inquiry. The president of the board was a Wing Commander, a Squadron Leader was the Tornado expert, a well-qualified flying instructor, and an engineering officer would offer any further advice on the crash that he could discover from the wreckage. The president and his board were also happy to see that we were both alive.

But now I vividly recall a comment made to me years before after a flying accident took place at the base where I had once been stationed. I remember I was told that as an RAF pilot the worst thing I could possibly do if my aircraft crashed was to survive.

I gave my evidence to the board of inquiry, as did Rob. At that time I was convinced that something had gone very badly wrong with the control systems of our aircraft. It had simply gone out of control and

209

there was nothing I could have done to prevent the accident.

I felt terribly sorry for Rob. He faced a three-month wait before he stood a chance of flying again. At least if I embarked on a decent fitness course – and my recovery rate from any illness or injury had always been good – I should be flying in a matter of weeks.

Only a week or so later I was discharged from hospital after being pronounced fit. I returned to my base and went along to the flight simulator, where I flew an exhausting and demanding emergencies check mission. I then reported to my Squadron Commander that I was now fit to fly. Then came the bombshell. I was told I would not be allowed to fly as the captain of a Tornado. I could fly only if I was accompanied by another pilot of at least the same rank as myself. Effectively, we would have to find a trainer aircraft with controls in both cockpits and another Squadron Leader would assume command from the rear seat. These requirements meant that I would probably only be in a position to fly a fast jet about once or twice a month.

But if I did manage to arrange both the jet and a fellow officer for the event, he would be coming along as my nursemaid. Of course, for all to see, I was guilty of being responsible for that crash until I could be proved innocent.

It made my position as a training officer on a front-line Tornado squadron in northern Germany absolutely untenable. The boss tried to persuade me that this restriction was normal for any aircrew member who had been involved in a crash. He would never be allowed to fly as a captain of another aircraft until all the findings of the accident had been completed. This, I know, was utterly untrue. Only months before my accident, a Phantom pilot based at Wildenrath had ejected from his jet, having lost control. He admitted to the investigators that it had been entirely down to his own flawed judgement. In the RAF that kind of mistake is known as negligence. But within weeks of ejecting from an aircraft and having admitted pilot error, the Phantom pilot was flying again. However, for the next six months, the very last six months of my career, I was to be slowly spit-roasted.

As the board of inquiry regularly called me back to offer further evidence, it became clear that my views and recollections would be brushed aside, or, worse, exploited to prove my own guilt. Whatever I said, any evidence that could be found to support a case for pilot mishandling was almost certainly seized upon. Even some of the airmen who had previously worked on that wrecked jet had hinted at problems. But their jobs were on the line as well, and I couldn't ask any of them to risk them for my sake.

In early August I was finally posted to RAF Cottesmore in Rutland for the final stretch of my career. I was not posted in any executive capacity but I was there to help me carry out my final civilian resettlement courses.

On 5 November I was finally recalled to Germany to be interviewed by the Commander in Chief of Royal Air Force Germany, Sir Andrew Wilson, about the findings of the board of inquiry. He told me that I had narrowly avoided a court martial. I didn't find the nerve to tell him that I had been pushing for a court hearing. At least then, I would have been innocent until these people could prove that I had been guilty of negligence. I had spent the last six months already regarded as guilty, whereas I had been hoping to be able to prove my innocence.

There was also a crushing coincidence attached to my final visit to RAF Germany on 5 November. At the very same RAF Rheindahlen mess where I changed into my number one uniform to be inter- viewed by the Commander, in adjoining rooms other officers were changing into theirs. But they were there to receive the fresh ribbons and accolades bestowed upon them for the time they had served in the Gulf. If it was just a coincidence, it was a very painful one. If it was someone's cruel idea of sticking the knife in, they had done a very good job.

I felt almost persecuted during my last six months as a serving RAF officer. Many of my colleagues had told me that everyone who is involved in an air crash goes through the mill. But I had decided I would fight to prove my innocence.

I am still not sure what terrible thing, in the RAF's eyes, I did during the Gulf War or after, but my conscience remains clear. I had already made my decision to leave the RAF in June 1990. If I hadn't then been promoted to Squadron Leader, I would have left eighteen months before that. If there hadn't been a war I would have gone in June 1991.

I was the right side of forty then, and felt it was time to try the world outside. My greatest dream was to land a job as a civilian pilot. Then I could really say

I had done it all: from helicopters to fast jets and then jumbo jets.

I had already lived on borrowed time for a number of years on Tornado squadrons. The average age for a fighter pilot is certainly no more than thirty, and I had been on the wrong side of that for eleven years.

But now I am very sad to have left the RAF under such a cloud. I just hope in the years to come, when I have had time to think and perhaps to forgive, I'll be able to look back on the many great years as a happy, contented and loyal officer.

Shortly after getting back from the Gulf, I was approached by the BBC to be one of their main subjects in a documentary about life after the war. I was delighted to take part but first I asked for the blessing and support of the MoD and the RAF. That support was given and I understood that the report which appeared on the television contained nothing controversial that would have adversely affected the RAF or any of its serving staff or their families. However, the station bosses in Germany took grave offence at the programme and suggested I had been nothing less than insensitive to the feelings of other servicemen who had been in the Gulf, and to their families.

One evening shortly after, my wife, Sheila, was admonished like a schoolchild by the Wing Commander in charge of Operations at Laarbruch. He told her that we had shown little or no compassion for those who may be angry and hurt about my willingness to appear in the programme, which was seen in my home town of Birmingham. We were astonished and staggered by this reactionary attitude to some very tame piece of journalism that did no one any harm and perhaps did the RAF publicity machine a great deal of good.

The pressure upon me became even greater when I dared to go the whole way and tell my story to a national newspaper. That certainly carried me right down the road to becoming an outcast from the service.

The stories that I told to the public are mine. I have not stolen anyone's thunder or plagiarized their experiences. But I have lost many friends for daring to speak out and tell it like it really was. Sadly, I lost the friendship of John Peters and of John Nichol over this. Perhaps that was because they must endure years of this unreasonable peer pressure before their careers come to an end.

I am not certain that I could have tolerated a moment longer of this cover-up, restraint and pressure to always do things the RAF way. Those officers who have no choice but to carry on doing things the RAF way are welcome to it. I would have spoken out and told my story even if I had been twenty years younger.

I just ask that the men I still respect and feel immensely proud of stop resenting me because I have decided to tell the world about the war that I fought. I had made my plans to leave a long time ago. The war made that an irrevocable decision. There could have been no going back after what I had lived through.

At least the war came for me at the end of a successful and enjoyable military career. I feel sorry for many of those young men for whom it came at the beginning of their careers. I am not sure what they have got to look forward to now. Already my XV Squadron has been disbanded and many others have gone in the wake of a new peace in Europe.

I have listened to countless youngsters who would now like to leave the service but fear the recession will leave them jobless, with no career at all. They have told me they want to leave because they feel let down, disappointed and rejected by the service. I just hope the RAF finally realizes that many of these good young men, the senior officers of tomorrow, will leave unless the loyalty they have shown to the service is reciprocated. They, like me, have helped to make history, and that should never be forgotten.

Many of my friends who are now in civilian life have told me of the remorse they felt at leaving the service. They were reluctant to finally go and showed a great willingness to renew old acquaintances and meet up with other ex-servicemen whenever they could.

But I counted every day as a day closer to the time when I could finally leave the RAF behind me. There is no chance that I would have wanted to stay on and I know the RAF no longer had any room for me.

During the three months between crashing my jet in northern Germany and leaving my base there for England, my Station Commander never spoke to me until my departure interview. Nor did he find the time to speak to Rob Woods. There had been no words of relief that we had survived, or any comforting talks

215

with our wives. Somehow, to speak to us would have tarnished him with our guilt of having been involved in an air crash.

But the fact is that I am alive and my navigator is alive and we did not harm one other person on the ground. We just burnt a bit of a corner of a German wood.

I only ever flew one more sortie in a Tornado after that dreadful crash. On 2 July, with Gordon Buckley as the captain, I enjoyed my last flight for the Royal Air Force. I am grateful to him for sitting in the back seat and not once touching the dual controls or handing out instructions to me. He made my last flight as painless as possible. It was a kind gesture.

I was never once allowed to prove my ability again or restore my confidence in myself. Someone had simply decided I was no longer fit to take the controls, but no one ever explained to me why.

I was invited to the final disbandment parade of XV Squadron on 10 December. I believed that going would have been a final act of defiance on my part. For sure, it would have already been a very sad affair after so many fine years as one of the most notable RAF squadrons. I didn't want to be a focus of attention at that final and glorious hour.

RAF squadrons in their colours, in their battle honours, are bigger than any single person or any group of people. XV Squadron will long outlive the memory of any Squadron Commander, good or bad. It still deserves my loyalty and it wholeheartedly has it.

# Appendix

## Pablo's War

*Record of Gulf War Missions
Flown by Squadron Leader Pablo Mason,
XV Squadron RAF*

The details of each mission are presented in a standard layout and offer the facts, with few frills. Some aspects are intentionally vague, to avoid offering up official secrets for general consumption. Many of the techniques we used are unlikely to be modified much for the next 'bash'. As for precise place-names, most of them are unpronounceable and would mean little to the reader. I have attempted to keep jargon to a fair minimum while retaining the style of a combat report; and while most of the subheadings should be self-explanatory, I will elaborate on a few points.

*Mission:*

We saw the prime objective of every mission we flew as being to survive. A 'singleton' aircraft would stand little chance of survival, against both air threats and target defences. Too small a formation would offer little protection and too large a formation would become unwieldy.

A four-aircraft formation had proved over the years to be the optimum size for our type of mission. If the weapons effects desired over a specific target called for more aircraft, the simple answer was to send multiples of four at acceptable intervals. Several attempts were made to reinvent the wheel!

*Type of attack:*
'Medium-level' means any height from a few hundred feet to as high as we could go. We varied altitude as much as possible to keep the Iraqis guessing. Sometimes we would dive on to a target, which usually made for greater accuracy and increased punch, but it tended to give the Triple A batteries more of a sporting chance! When the Buccaneers joined us and we began laser-guided bombing, attaining weapons accuracy became far less of a problem. The Tornado could carry a maximum of either three laser-guided or eight standard 1000-lb bombs under the fuselage.

*Airborne time:*
We would usually be strapped into our cockpits, with all systems checked and ready for engine start, about one hour before take-off. Final sortie preparation would have been going on for at least three or four hours before that. A detailed mission plan would often have taken another four hours to produce, regardless of the planned sortie duration. Thus some nine hours would have been devoted to a mission by the aircrew, before actually becoming airborne. After landing, the aircraft shut-down

checks and subsequent engineering hand-over would take about an hour; and then the intricate mission debrief would follow as soon as possible. If we were lucky and the mission had been fairly straightforward, we could be out of the debrief within two or three hours. So, while all I have logged is the airborne time, each mission would most certainly have had well over twelve hours devoted to it.

*Mission support:*
Invariably the number of aircraft directly supporting a Tornado ground-attack mission would well exceed the number of Tornadoes involved in it. Our air-to-air refuelling support was always provided by the RAF, either by the aged Victor tankers or the more modern VC10s. Both outfits provided a superb service, although there were occasional glitches.

The Americans provided all the rest of our airborne support and were always magnificent. The airborne warning and control system (AWACS) was there without fail, a highly modified airliner crammed with electronic wizardry, giving reassuring 'picture clean' calls and offering instant evaluations of possible threats which came up on its radar scopes. Our fighter escorts were most often F 15 Eagles, which could turn on a sixpence and climb vertically with a full weapon load. They were always spoiling for a fight, and I almost felt sorry that they rarely got one.

Other specialist support aircraft were usually

much more productively employed. Some could make enemy radar screens look as though they had been completely whitewashed. There were the anti-missile boys who would go about tempting SAM and Triple A systems to lock them up on their acquisition radars. A few seconds later an unwitting Iraqi radar operator would probably be suffering from a Mach 2 enema, in the form of an anti-radar missile!

*Approximate routing:*

Our flight paths through Allied airspace were usually planned along 'safe lanes' which were known to all, and changed regularly. Once inside enemy airspace, or 'Sausage Side', our route was up to us. We avoided known and prebriefed threat areas and complained frequently about the lack of up-to-the-minute intelligence. Gary and I preferred to fly a zigzag route, turning in towards our target as late as possible. This would keep the enemy guessing as to our final drop-off point, and we could easily cut corners if there was a need to amend our timing. Ensuring accurate timing over target was most important in order to guarantee deconfliction between aircraft. Sometimes we were part of some big daisy-chain of attackers, pounding away at a target for hours on end, and usually it would be Gary and I who opened the batting.

The run for home would invariably become a race, eyes out on stalks and balls to the wall.

*Weather:*

The Tornado GR 1 is well capable of all-weather

operations and blind bombing. However, for laser-guided bombing missions the weather over target needed to be good, otherwise the laser energy would become dispersed by cloud, rain or smoke and would fail to guide the bombs.

## Thursday 17 January 1991

*Mission:*
  To lead an attack by four Tornadoes on a military airfield in south-eastern Iraq

*Type of attack:*
  Day, ultra-low-level, with 8×1000-lb high-explosive bombs each, attacking from the west

*Airborne time:*
  4 hours day flying

*Mission support:*
  American EA 6 Prowler and F 18 Hornet for SAM defence suppression; RAF Victor tankers; AWACS

*Approximate routing:*
  North-west from Muharraq into Saudi Arabia for 500 miles, then north into Iraq, turning north-east and finally on to east. Recovery routing: reciprocal

*Weather:*
  Gin-clear, no cloud, unlimited visibility

*Observations en route:*
  Evidence of earlier air strikes on enemy installations

*Target observations:*
Heavy Triple A and SAM activity

*Remarks:*
First Tornado GR 1 daylight mission of the war. Formation reduced to three because of aircraft unserviceability. Flt Lts Peters and Nichol (number two) shot down during escape manoeuvre off target

*Notes:* pp. 16–25

## Sunday 20 January 1991

*Mission:*
To lead an attack by eight Tornadoes and disrupt enemy operations from a military airfield 80 miles south of Baghdad

*Type of attack:*
Day into night, medium-level, with 8×1000-lb high-explosive bombs each, attacking from the south-west

*Airborne time:*
30 minutes day flying; $3^{1}/_{2}$ hours night flying

*Mission support:*
American EF 111 Raven electronic jammer and F 14 Tomcat for SAM defence suppression; RAF Victor tankers; fighter escort; AWACS

*Approximate routing:*
North-west from Muharraq into Saudi Arabia for

500 miles, then north into Iraq. Zigzag in to target, then run out south

*Weather:*
Clear skies, mist/fog in target area, no moon

*Observations en route:*
Nil significant. Slight confusion during air-to-air refuelling homebound

*Target observations:*
Systems failures during run in to target necessitated position changes and close-formation weapons release. No reaction from target defences until first weapons impact, then very heavy tracer and airburst fire, mostly below the formation. Little SAM activity observed. Avoided mosque to north of target

*Remarks:*
First Tornado GR 1 night medium-level mission of the war

*Notes:* pp. 88–95

## Monday 21 January 1991

*Mission:*
To lead an attack by sixteen Tornadoes and disrupt enemy operations from a military airfield 80 miles west of Basrah, Iraq

*Type of attack:*
Night, medium-level, with 8×1000-lb high-explosive

bombs each, attacking from the west in close formation

*Airborne time:*
4 hours 20 minutes night flying; $1^1/_2$ hours in cloud

*Mission support:*
American F 4 Phantom Wild Weasel for SAM defence suppression; American F 15 Eagle fighter escort; RAF VC10 and Victor tankers; AWACS

*Approximate routing:*
North-west from Muharraq into Saudi Arabia for 400 miles, then north-east into Iraq and finally on to east. Recovery routing: initially south-west, then south for Saudi Arabia

*Weather:*
Clear over target, cloud en route, some moonlight

*Observations en route:*
Sporadic SAM activity, possible enemy fighter activity during run out

*Target observations:*
Little action until first weapons impact, then very heavy tracer, airburst fire and SAM activity. Also heavy Triple A fire from south-east. Large convoy moving in towards target from north-west

*Remarks:*
Flt Lt Cobb and Fg Off Wilson (number six) turned back before target and engaged target of opportunity in Iraq. Missile alert during recovery to Muharraq

*Notes:* pp. 155–162

## Friday 25 January 1991

*Mission:*
To lead an attack by eight Tornadoes and destroy an oil pumping station in south-eastern Iraq, 75 miles north of Kuwait City

*Type of attack:*
Night into day, medium-level, with 8×1000-lb high-explosive bombs each, attacking from the east

*Airborne time:*
$1^1/_2$ hours night flying; 30 minutes day flying

*Mission support:*
American F 4 Phantom Wild Weasel for SAM defence suppression; American F 15 Eagle fighter escort; American EF 111 Raven electronic jammer (withdrawn at late stage in planning); RAF Victor tankers; AWACS

*Approximate routing:*
North along Saudi Arabian coast, then skirt Iraq–Iran border to attack from east. Run out south-east

*Weather:*
Slight haze, some lower cloud, pleasant sunrise

*Observations en route:*
Sporadic Triple A fire from coastal emplacements

*Target observations:*
Heavy Triple A fire, mostly just below formation but some overhead. Several secondary explosions and much flying debris

*Remarks:*
Withdrawal of EF 11 caused some concern. Target burned for four days. Two aircraft turned back with kit problems before target. Slight problems finding tankers homebound

*Notes:* pp. 71–6

## Monday 28 January 1991

*Mission:*
To lead the rear element of four Tornadoes in an attack by ten Tornadoes on a petroleum refinery 120 miles south-east of Baghdad

*Type of attack:*
Night, medium-level, with $8 \times 1000$-lb high-explosive bombs each, attacking from the south-west

*Airborne time:*
$3^1/_2$ hours night flying

*Mission support:*
American F 4 Phantom Wild Weasel for SAM defence suppression; American F 15 Eagle fighter escort; RAF Victor tankers; AWACS

*Approximate routing:*
North-west from Muharraq into Saudi Arabia for

400 miles, then north into Iraq, turning north-east
on to target. Initially south-east off target, then
south for Saudi Arabia

*Weather:*
Clear skies, excellent visibility, full moon

*Observations en route:*
Turbulence during air-to-air refuelling. Light Triple
A fire from enemy airfields

*Target observations:*
Large secondary explosions

*Remarks:*
Target burned for two days

*Notes:*pp. 162–4


## 30 January–1 February 1991

*Missions (× 3):*
To refine and develop tactics for delivery of laser-
guided munitions from low and medium level

*Type of attacks:*
Daylight, level and shallow dive, formation size
increasing with expertise

*Airborne time:*
6 hours day flying (three sorties)

*Mission support:*
RAF Buccaneer 'pave-spikers'; RAF Victor tankers

*Approximate routing:*
'Mirror'-style sorties in the desert, leading to simulated attack profiles in Saudi Arabia and Bahrain

*Weather:*
Good visibility

*Observations en route:*
Nil

*Target observations:*
Allied bridges, installations and airfields selected
to simulate, as closely as possible, enemy targets

*Remarks:*
Tactics developed and presented to Detachment
Commander and formation leaders for consider-
ation and dissemination

*Notes:* p. 96


## Saturday 2 February 1991

*Mission:*
To lead an attack by four Tornadoes and three
Buccaneers on a highway bridge over the River
Euphrates 120 miles south of Baghdad

*Type of attack:*
Day, medium-level, with 3×1000-lb laser-guided
high-explosive bombs each Tornado, attacking
from the south-west

*Airborne time:*
$3^1/_2$ hours day flying; 1 hour in cloud

*Mission support:*
American F 15 Eagle fighter escort; RAF VC10 tankers; AWACS

*Approximate routing:*
North-west from Muharraq into Saudi Arabia for 500 miles, then north into Iraq. Zigzag into target, turning left on to south-west, then south for Saudi Arabia

*Weather:*
Clear skies over target, substantial medium-level cloud en route to within 50 miles of target

*Observations en route:*
Close formation flown in cloud over enemy territory, with sporadic indications of SAM radar acquisitions (most uncomfortable!)

*Target observations:*
Target destroyed, with several spans completely missing. Light Triple A fire, mostly below the formation, from town 5 miles south

*Remarks:*
First Tornado GR 1 laser-guided bombing mission of the war. One extra Buccaneer flown as airborne spare, which was not required and returned to base without entering enemy airspace

*Notes:* pp. 96–8

## Monday 4 February 1991

*Mission:*
To lead an attack by four Tornadoes and two

Buccaneers on a highway bridge over the River Euphrates 40 miles north-west of Basrah

*Type of attack:*
Day, medium-level, with 3×1000-lb laser-guided high-explosive bombs each Tornado, attacking from the east

*Airborne time:*
2 hours day flying

*Mission support:*
American EF 111 Raven electronic jammer and F 4 Phantom Wild Weasel for SAM defence suppression; roving American fighter Combat Air Patrols; RAF Victor tankers; AWACS

*Approximate routing:*
North along Saudi Arabian coast, then hug Iraq–Iran border to attack from east. Turn left off target, back along border and down the Gulf

*Weather:*
Crystal-clear, fresh northerly wind

*Observations en route:*
Considerable evidence of destruction and damage to enemy installations. Sporadic light Triple A fire

*Target observations:*
Northern and southern spans destroyed; two lorries left on centre span. Light Triple A fire from town on southern bank.

*Remarks:*
The world-famous video!

## *Wednesday 6 February 1991*

*Mission:*
  To lead an attack by eight Tornadoes and disrupt
  enemy operations from a military airfield 80 miles
  south-east of Baghdad

*Type of attack:*
  Day, medium-level, with 4×1000-lb high-explosive
  bombs each, attacking from the south

*Airborne time:*
  $3^1/_4$ hours day flying; 20 minutes in cloud

*Mission support:*
  American F 4 Phantom Wild Weasel for SAM
  defence suppressions; American F 15 Eagle fighter
  escort; RAF Victor tankers; AWACS

*Approximate routing:*
  North-west from Muharraq into Saudi Arabia for
  400 miles, then zigzag into Iraq, splitting the
  formation to attack simultaneously from several
  directions. Run out south into Saudi Arabia

*Weather:*
  Thick, medium-level cloud

*Observations en route:*
  Some enemy radar activity but nothing seen

*Target observations:*
  Target obscured by cloud. Attacked using aircraft
  radar. Light Triple A fire after first weapons
  impact

*Remarks:*
Felt uncomfortable flying so close to the cloud tops, which would have delayed reaction to SAM sightings

## Friday 8 February 1991

*Mission:*
To lead an attack by four Tornadoes and two Buccaneers on a highway bridge over the River Euphrates 45 miles west of Baghdad

*Type of attack:*
Night into day, medium-level, with $3 \times 1000$-lb laser-guided high-explosive bombs each Tornado, attacking from the south

*Airborne time:*
20 minutes night flying; 4 hours day flying

*Mission support:*
American F 4 Phantom Wild Weasel and EF 111 Raven electronic jammer for SAM defence suppression; American F 15 Eagle fighter escort; RAF VC10 tankers; AWACS

*Approximate routing:*
North-west into Saudi Arabia for 550 miles, then zigzag into Iraq and finally on to north for the target. Run out south-west, then south for Saudi Arabia

*Weather:*
Layered cloud over Saudi Arabia but fine over target

*Observations en route:*
   Acquired and engaged by SAM 2 and SAM 3
   missile systems, which were evaded

*Target observations:*
   Heavy damage but still usable. Barrage of Triple
   A fire from town to the south-east. Triple A fire
   over target lighter than anticipated

*Notes:* pp. 101–2

## Saturday 9 February 1991

*Mission:*
   To lead the rear element of four Tornadoes in an
   attack by eight Tornadoes on a petroleum storage
   site 170 miles south-east of Baghdad

*Type of attack:*
   Day, dive from medium level through broken
   cloud, with 4×1000-lb high-explosive bombs each,
   attacking from the south-east

*Airborne time:*
   2 hours 10 minutes day flying

*Mission support:*
   American F 4 Phantom Wild Weasel for SAM
   defence suppression; American Navy F 14 Tomcat
   fighter escort; RAF Victor tankers; AWACS

*Approximate routing:*
   North along Saudi Arabian coast, then north-west
   between Kuwait and Iran. Turn right off target to
   run south-east for the Gulf

*Weather:*
Approximately half cloud cover over target

*Observations en route:*
Surface mostly obscured by low cloud

*Target observations:*
Good hits by leading element. Flew through cloud and moderate Triple A fire to ensure better acquisition

*Remarks:*
On reflection, rather silly

*Notes:* p. 102–3

## Sunday 10 February 1991

*Mission:*
To lead an attack by four Tornadoes and two Buccaneers on a highway bridge over the River Euphrates 45 miles west of Baghdad

*Type of attack:*
Night into day, medium-level, with 3×1000-lb laser-guided high-explosive bombs each Tornado, attacking from the south-west

*Airborne time:*
20 minutes night flying; 4 hours day flying

*Mission support:*
American F 4 Phantom Wild Weasel and EF 111 Raven electronic jammer for SAM defence

suppression; roving American fighter Combat Air
Patrols; RAF VC 10 tankers; AWACS

*Approximate routing:*
North-west into Saudi Arabia for 550 miles, then
zigzag into Iraq and finally on to north-east for
target. Turn left off target to run out south-west,
then south for Saudi Arabia

*Weather:*
Clear skies, fresh north-westerly winds

*Observations en route:*
Evidence of destruction and damage to enemy
installations, several fires. Sporadic indications of
SAM activity; nothing seen

*Target observations:*
Target obscured by thick smoke from burning oil
refinery to the north-west. SAMs, seen to launch
from site to east of target, engaged and destroyed
by F 4s. Moderate Triple A fire from airfield west
of target

## Monday 11 February 1991

*Mission:*
To lead an attack by four Tornadoes and two
Buccaneers on a highway bridge over the River
Tigris 80 miles north-west of Basrah

*Type of attack:*
Day, medium-level into shallow dive, with 3×1000-
lb laser-guided high-explosive bombs each Tornado,
attacking from the south-east

*Airborne time:*
   2 hours day flying

*Mission support:*
   American EF 111 Raven electronic jammer and
   F 4 Phantom Wild Weasel for SAM defence
   suppression; roving American F 15 Eagle fighter
   Combat Air Patrols

*Approximate routing:*
   North along Saudi Arabian coast, then hug Iraq–Iran
   border to attack from south-east. Turn right off target
   and reciprocal route home

*Weather:*
   Excellent visibility, light wind

*Observations en route:*
   Hardly any Triple A or SAM activity. Personal
   Locator Beacon transmission received and details
   passed to AWACS controller

*Target observations:*
   Vehicles and personnel on bridge. Smoke and
   debris as a result of direct hits from leading
   element obscured target from trailing element.
   Bridge severely damaged

*Notes:* pp. 80–2

## Wednesday 13 February 1991

*Mission:*
   To lead an attack by four Tornadoes and two
   Buccaneers and disrupt enemy operations from

two military airfields 40 miles west and 110 miles west of Baghdad

*Type of attack:*
Day, medium-level, with 3×1000-lb laser-guided high-explosive bombs each Tornado, attacking first target from the south-west and second target from the east.

*Airborne time:*
4$^1/_4$ hours day flying

*Mission support:*
American EF 111 and F 4 Phantom for SAM defence suppression; roving American F 15 Eagle fighter Combat Air Patrols; RAF VC10 tanker

*Approximate routing:*
North-west from Muharraq into Saudi Arabia for 600 miles, then zigzag into Iraq and finally on to north-east for first target. Turn left off target to run in for second target heading north-west. Turn left off target to run south for Saudi Arabia

*Weather:*
Slight haze

*Observations en route:*
Infrequent indications of SAM activity; nothing seen. One allied ground-attack aircraft (Hunter 26) engaged by enemy Triple A/SAM and downed

*Target observations:*
Weapons retained at first target and missed the second. Moderate to heavy Triple A fire overhead

both targets but mostly below aircraft. Some SAM firings, apparently unguided

*Remarks:*

A very complex task. Believed to be the only mission involving Tornado GR 1s against two enemy airfields in one sortie. First war sortie for Buccaneer crews.

*Notes:* pp. 118–25

## Thursday 14 February 1991

*Mission:*

To lead an attack by eight Tornadoes and four Buccaneers and destroy hardened aircraft shelters on a military airfield 40 miles west of Baghdad

*Type of attack:*

Day, medium-level into shallow dive, with 2×1000-lb laser-guided high-explosive bombs each Tornado, attacking from the west

*Airborne time:*

4 hours 20 minutes day flying

*Mission support:*

American EF 111 Raven electronic jammer and F 4 Phantom Wild Weasel for SAM defence suppression; roving American F 15 Eagle fighter Combat Air Patrols; RAF VC10 tankers; AWACS

*Approximate routing:*

North-west from Muharraq into Saudi Arabia for 600 miles, then zigzag north into Iraq to attack from west. Initial heading north-west off target, then run-out south for Saudi Arabia

*Weather:*
Thick, medium-level cloud en route, clear skies over target

*Observations en route:*
Some difficulty during air-to-air refuelling, due to turbulence and cloud. Rear elements of formation unsuccessfully engaged by SAMs during approach to target

*Target observations:*
Heavy Triple A from sites around the airfield. Several SAM firings. Flt Lts Clark and Hicks (number eleven) shot down over target, probably by SAM 3. Several aircraft shelters destroyed by direct hits

*Notes:* pp. 126–9

## Sunday 17 February 1991

*Mission:*
To lead an attack by four Tornadoes and two Buccaneers against hardened aircraft shelters on an airfield 120 miles south-east of Baghdad

*Type of attack:*
Day, medium-level, with 2×1000-lb laser-guided high-explosive bombs each Tornado, attacking from the south-west

*Airborne time:*
2 hours 20 minutes day flying; 1 hour in cloud

*Mission support:*
American F 4 Phantom and EF 111 for SAM defence suppression; American F 18 Hornet fighter escort; AWACS

*Approximate routing:*
North along Saudi Arabian coast, then close and parallel to Iraq–Iran border before a 120-mile zigzag into target. Straight ahead off target, then turn right to run out south-east for the Gulf

*Weather:*
Slight haze en route, cloud over target area and much of Iraq

*Observations en route:*
Very little enemy activity

*Target observations:*
Mission-support aircraft gave warning of SAM 3 in target area but nothing seen. Cloud partially obscured target

## Wednesday 20 February 1991

*Mission:*
To lead an attack by four Tornadoes and two Buccaneers against the runway surface of a military airfield in south-eastern Iraq

*Type of attack:*
Day, medium-level, with 2×1000-lb laser-guided high-explosive bombs each aircraft, attacking from the north-west

*Airborne time:*
2 hours 5 minutes day flying; 30 minutes in cloud

*Mission support:*
American F 4 Phantom Wild Weasel and EF 111 Raven electronic jammer for SAM defence suppression; American F 18 Hornet fighter escort; AWACS

*Approximate routing:*
North along Saudi Arabian coast, then hug Iraq–Iran border for 100 miles. Skirt known defences to the north of target and attack heading south-east. Turn north-east off target and reacquire border to run south-east for the Gulf

*Weather:*
Thick cloud, with embedded thunder clouds, from low level to 20–30,000ft (as forecast!)

*Observations en route:*
Able to remain above cloud for part of route. Numerous indications of SAM radars, particularly around Basrah; nothing seen

*Target observations:*
Obscured by thick thunder cloud. Weapons retained

*Remarks:*
Weather forecast for target area totally unsuitable for laser operations. Requests for change of weapon load or cancellation of mission refused. *Why?*

## Friday 22 February 1991

*Mission:*
To lead an attack by four Tornadoes and two Buccaneers against the main runway of a military airfield 120 miles south-east of Baghdad

*Type of attack:*
Day, medium-level, with 3×1000-lb laser-guided high-explosive bombs each Tornado and 2×1000-lb laser-guided bombs each Buccaneer, attacking simultaneously from different directions

*Airborne time:*
2 hours 20 minutes day flying

*Mission support:*
American F 4 Phantom Wild Weasel for SAM defence suppression; roving American F 14 Tomcat fighter Combat Air Patrols

*Approximate routing:*
North along Saudi Arabian coast, then close and parallel to Iraq–Iran border before a 60-mile run into target. Regroup off target to depart south-east for the Gulf

*Weather:*
No significant cloud, good visibility

*Observations en route:*
Very quiet. Oil fires over Kuwait

*Target observations:*
On completion of Tornado attacks, Buccaneers

attacked in high-angle, self-designated dive. Very heavy damage achieved to several segments of runway surface. Hardly any Triple A or SAM activity

## Saturday 23 February 1991

*Mission:*
To lead an attack by four Tornadoes and two Buccaneers against the main runway and taxiway of an airfield 130 miles south-east of Baghdad

*Type of attack:*
Early-morning, medium-level, with 2×1000-lb laser-guided high-explosive bombs each aircraft, attacking from the south-east

*Airborne time:*
2 hours 10 minutes day flying

*Mission support:*
American F 4 Phantom Wild Weasel for SAM defence suppression; roving American F 15 Eagle fighter Combat Air Patrols; AWACS

*Approximate routing:*
North along Saudi Arabian coast, then north-west between Kuwait and Iran. Zigzag into attack heading north-west. Turn left off target and reciprocal route home

*Weather:*
No cloud, unlimited visibility

*Observations en route:*
Burning Kuwaiti oilfields visible for several hundred miles. Some enemy ground activity close to Iraqi border. Light Triple A fire around Basrah

*Target observations:*
Extremely quiet. Excellent bombing results, mostly direct hits

*Notes:* pp. 165–6

## Monday 25 February 1991

*Mission:*
To lead an attack by four Tornadoes and two Buccaneers and disrupt enemy operations from a military airfield 40 miles west of Baghdad

*Type of attack:*
Day, medium-level, with 2×1000-lb laser-guided high-explosive bombs each Tornado, attacking from the west and north-west

*Airborne time:*
4 hours 10 minutes day flying; 2 hours in cloud

*Mission support:*
American EF 111 Raven electronic jammer and F 4 Phantom Wild Weasel for SAM defence suppresssion; roving American F 15 Eagle fighter Combat Air Patrols: RAF Victor tanker; AWACS

*Approximate routing:*
North-west from Muharraq into Saudi Arabia for 600 miles, then zigzag, progressing north into

Iraq to pass west abeam target before turning in to attack. Turn right off target to run south for Saudi Arabia

*Weather:*
Thick, turbulent cloud with embedded thunder cloud from low level to 20–30,000ft. (As forecast by Met Office and observed by previous missions!)

*Observations en route:*
Poor weather conditions demanded close-formation flying for long periods. Flying in close formation in cloud over Iraq, with a warning of attack by SAMs, is a guaranteed cure for constipation!

*Target observations:*
Obscured by thick cloud. Weapons retained

*Remarks:*
Repeated requests for change of weapon load or cancellation of mission denied by Headquarters

*Notes:* pp. 167–70

| | | | |
|---|---|---|---|
| ☐ | Don't Cry For Me, Sergeant Major | Jeremy Hands and Bob McGowan | £4.99 |
| ☐ | Try Not To Laugh, Sergeant Major | Jeremy Hands and Bob McGowan | £4.99 |
| ☐ | Kiss The Boys Goodbye | Monika Jensen-Stevenson | £6.99 |
| ☐ | 2 Para Falklands | Major-General John Frost | £3.50 |
| ☐ | Men of the Red Beret | Max Arthur | £6.99 |
| ☐ | Combat Crew | John Comer | £5.99 |
| ☐ | The Falklands War | *Sunday Times* Insight Team | £5.99 |

Warner Books now offers an exciting range of quality titles by both established and new authors which can be ordered from the following address:

Little, Brown and Company (UK),
P.O. Box 11,
Falmouth,
Cornwall TR10 9EN.

Alternatively you may fax your order to the above address.
Fax No. 0326 376423.

Payments can be made as follows: cheque, postal order (payable to Little, Brown and Company) or by credit cards, Visa/Access. Do not send cash or currency. UK customers and B.F.P.O. please allow £1.00 for postage and packing for the first book, plus 50p for the second book, plus 30p for each additional book up to a maximum charge of £3.00 (7 books plus).

Overseas customers including Ireland please allow £2.00 for the first book plus £1.00 for the second book, plus 50p for each additional book.

NAME  (Block Letters) ......................................................

..................................................................................

ADDRESS ....................................................................

..................................................................................

..................................................................................

☐ I enclose my remittance for ...........................................

☐ I wish to pay by Access/Visa Card

Number ☐☐☐☐☐☐☐☐☐☐☐☐☐☐☐☐

Card Expiry Date ☐☐☐☐